ROSLYN RICE ENDORSEMENTS

"As I started reading this book, immediately I was arrested by its content. I thought about how one word from Jesus: "Come" caused Peter to walk on the water. I also reflected back on my life and remembered the times when one word enabled me not only to survive the storms of life, but arrive safely on the other side of it.

This is a powerful, insightful and life changing book. Roslyn did an amazing job with sharing her personal stories that made the book come alive and become applicable for the times we are living in. I highly recommend this book for everyone regardless of your religion preferences. This book will change your life."

—Tony Douglas
International Bestselling Author of
Discerning the Voice of God by the Leading of the Holy Spirit

"*The Power of One* is a striking account of Roslyn Rice's journey of faith. Taking the readers on a spiritual journey with her, Roslyn shares intimate accounts of her life and the influence of one word from Jesus carrying her through the darkest periods in her life. It's a powerful reminder to reconnect with God and surrender fully to a higher being, having faith in the most desperate of moments."

—Peggy McColl
New York Times Bestselling Author

"Roslyn Rice writes an incredible book called *The Power of One* that will inspire you to go on your personal quest of finding faith. Exploring her relationship with Jesus and the impact of His words through various aspects of her life, this is a wonderful read that will help readers truly focus on the power of one word and how it has the ability to transform their lives."

—Judy O'Beirn
President & CEO of
Hasmark Publishing International

"Your message always resounds in my heart. I'm very encouraged by your one word. You are able to take feelings, thoughts, experiences and help me see them through the word of the Lord. Thank you!"

—A Recent Widow

POWER
of
ONE

FINDING HOPE IN THE MIDST OF STRUGGLE

Roslyn Rice

Hasmark
PUBLISHING
INTERNATIONAL

DEDICATION

To my mother, my queen, who sparked my love of words and instilled confidence.

To my forever (Tyjuan), thank you for never doubting my potential and hugging me on some of life's toughest days.

To my wombmate (Renee), we were knit together for such a time as this.

To Tyler and Joshua, your lives confidently keep me moving forward.

TABLE OF CONTENTS

FOREWORD

⌒

Being the author's identical twin sister means I've had the extreme pleasure of knowing her longer than anyone. For years Roslyn's been one of my largest supporters, confidantes, and accountability partners. She drips wisdom through her words that can support and challenge your state of being all in the same conversation.

When Roslyn shared with me that she was authoring a book about the power of one word, my heart leaped because words are powerful! Proverbs 18:21 shares that life and death are in the power of our tongues, the area of our body where words are given a voice. Our words help to articulate our innermost thoughts and desires of our hearts. Words have the power to inspire, encourage, and heal. They make a difference and can literally change the trajectory of your life.

Today as I write this foreword, I know the passion and intensity in which Roslyn authored this book. I also know that she's prayed and allowed the Holy Spirit to guide her selection of every word in her book. Buckle up and get ready to be blessed!

Renee R. Scott, CPCU, CLU

PREFACE

How do you bounce back after you've been reduced to zero?

How do you move forward when you are sitting in the uncomfortable seat of uncertainty?

How do you have peace after a scary medical diagnosis?

When you are disoriented by grief and loss, how do you start to heal?

How do you respond after betrayal?

What fuel do you use when you've spent years operating emotionally on empty?

You cling to the power of one word.

One word, spoken at the right time, can change the complete trajectory of your life.

One word that's simple enough for a grade school student to understand, yet powerful enough for a mature adult to harness its impact.

One word can awaken dreams that were buried for decades.

One word can provide a roadmap that propels you into a new stratosphere.

One word can shift your perspective. It can be an epiphany.

One word can reverse the residual effects of trauma and loss.

One word can provide complete peace in the midst of the storms of life.

One word can bring hope when you've been kicked in the gut.

It can breathe new life into a project or marriage that needs to be resurrected.

It can bring clarity to discern when to end and begin again.

It was the power of one word that saved my life.

I've always had an addiction to words. Writing has been a way to dump thoughts that are twirling around in my head. Words written and spoken are therapeutic for me.

I am intrigued by the way in which words can become building blocks for the most prolific speeches in history.

Words can inspire and uplift. They can also tear down and destroy. The power of one word narrows the focus. Words carry influence. One word becomes a north star to chart a new path forward. One word inspires. It also provides an anchor through turbulent times.

During times when you are hanging on for dear life or your back is up against a wall, there is no time for complex sentences and sermons. The wailing belted out from a heart of pain usually comes forth with only one word.

The power of one word from Jesus can calm and soothe the deepest and darkest pains in life.

The power of one provides direction when blinded eyes can't see.

The *Power of One* devotional is focused around words that carried me through some tough seasons of my life. Wilderness experiences in life are not welcome. They arrive unexpectedly. One word can trigger a new behavior or positive thought. One word jolts you into remembering God's promises. It awakens and refreshes you in the midst of a desert season. When life flattens you, the power of one word thrusts you back up again.

My prayer is that these simple yet power-packed words provide calm and just enough fresh air to get you moving again.

Prepare to be encouraged, equipped, and inspired by the power of one.

Romans 15:13 (NLT)

"I pray that God, the source of hope, will fill you completely with joy and peace because you trust in him.

Then you will overflow with confident hope through the power of the Holy Spirit."

INTRODUCTION

L ife can feel as if you are traveling on a road. You set out towards a destination and arrive at an intersection. There are days you will continue straight ahead. Other days you will make an abrupt turn. While living we have two roads intersecting at the same time. I've experienced days that are mountaintop experiences, such as celebrating my fifteenth wedding anniversary. I look over my shoulder wondering how long the euphoric feeling will last. While celebrating that anniversary, my son starts having a simple cough that turns into a fifty-day unknown illness with three trips to the ER—celebration and confusion intersecting at the same time.

We are all traveling life's arduous road experiencing the best and worst of times. It's an intersection of triumph and trials, grace and grief, struggle and success. You awaken to a normal day. Then a phone call delivers gut-wrenching news. Emotions fluctuate. Uncertainty appears. Fear settles in. Confusion lingers. Residual effects of that call last for years. During the darkest days of adversity, we search for a way to muster the strength to trust and be hopeful. When life throws a curveball, one word can contain all the capacity you possess to find hope. One simple word reminds you to keep moving forward.

Painful experiences make it tough to digest chapter scriptural readings. One word from God becomes more palatable.

During days of uncertainty, I've realized that an intentional dependence on God sustains. It centers me. It births confidence. Fear can close us off. Fear paralyzes. Fear creates a world that appears smaller and with fewer options. We embrace thoughts of the enemy when we walk in fear. Thoughts that we are not enough. Thoughts of abandonment and loneliness. Thoughts that devalue us. Thoughts that nudge us to throw in the towel and quit. What intersection are you at today?

Wherever the roads of life are intersecting for you today, God whispers. In times when I needed to hear Him most, it wasn't a full sentence or long dissertation. God provided one word. During life's travels we become distracted and drift off course. We veer off, chasing money or relationships. We long for acceptance from others. We crave perfection. The rat race of life leaves us breathless. The power of one word becomes a security blanket. When I am disoriented, one word transcends into a north star. One word whispered from God takes you new places. One word from God shifts a perspective. It provides new hope. It allows you to grow and evolve with grace.

Years ago, I started focusing on one word after the new year started. Instead of creating a list of failed resolutions, I found one word easier to digest. I replaced resolutions with one word. It provided a linear focus in every situation. It guided my efforts as the year ticked away. The freedom of one word was refreshing. I guided teams at work on selecting one word before they set annual goals. They quickly found that the one word wasn't just related to work. It converged into their personal life.

Each devotion in the book focuses on one word. Scriptures are shared that will reference the one word. At the end of each devotion, a question and prayer are provided to jumpstart the application of the word in your daily life. Unlike normal devotions, you might spend an unlimited amount of time mulling over and meditating on one word. Don't rush the process.

One word is a simple yet effective way to remember the promises of God. Ruminate on the one word until it penetrates your heart. Ponder the one word until you feel the weight lift off your shoulders. God does not need you to be strong through the storm. He longs for you to discern your weakness and need for Him.

One word has positively changed me. It's changed my outlook. It can do the same for you. Each devotion was a word ministered to me during one of the toughest years in history. A word to communicate hope arrived just when I needed it. *Power of One* will help you find hope in the midst of struggle. Embrace the simplicity of one word, because one word has the power to change the trajectory of your life.

If I were sitting with you today, I would ask how I could pray for you. Please accept this prayer from a sincere heart that wants you to experience the power of one word from God.

God, may You bless every reader. May they experience freedom from the pressures of life. Allow every word in this book to encourage. May each reader see You with fresh eyes. There is assurance to know that when we walk with You, we no longer walk in darkness (John 8:12). I pray they cling and gaze at the beauty of Your strength. Take away the desire to control, and release a spirit of surrender. May they wave the

white flag over their life. Restore faith. May each reader dis-
cover hope in You. Amen.

Romans 15:13 (NIV)

"May the God of hope fill you with all joy and peace as you
trust in him, so that you may overflow with hope by the power
of the Holy Spirit."

One word
has the
power to
change the
trajectory of
your life.

ROSLYN RICE

COURAGE

M y ten-year-old son experienced a medical condition that initially was unexplainable. I found myself in a hospital room zipping through hallways during the assessment phase of his hospital stay. The final room was one of seclusion because of a viral infection he'd developed. It was isolating. Everyone entering the room saw red warning signs about how contagious his infection was. Medical professionals entered only with hazmat suits on, which was a scary sight for us.

I was disoriented by the sequence of events. How does a ten-year-old go from healthy to sick in such a short amount of time? It was a confusing period for me. It was going to take courage to understand the next chapter. It also took courage when I sent that same son off to college years later. Today, it might take courage for you to slide out of bed and hope for a brighter day. Courage to parent that newborn while living in a total exhaustive state. Courage to make hard decisions about your aging parents. Courage to allow your young adult to make smart decisions. Courage to give the teenager the keys to the car. Courage to launch a new business. Courage to leave an abusive and toxic relationship. Courage to make the final decision to retire. Courage to begin life without that loved one who left Earth too soon.

Nelson Mandela said, "I learned that courage was not the absence of fear, but triumph over it. The brave man is not he who does not feel afraid, but he who conquers that fear." We have a choice: be paralyzed with fear or move forward with courage.

When I think of courage, I'm reminded of Moses in the Bible. He was chosen to lead the Israelites out of Egypt. Their enemy (Pharaoh and his army) chased them. They could hear the thunderous march of the chariots as they stood at the Red Sea. This sea was an obstacle preventing them from crossing to the other side, leaving oppression and slavery in the distance.

Exodus 14:10–14 (NLT)

"As Pharaoh approached, the people of Israel looked up and panicked when they saw the Egyptians overtaking them. They cried out to the Lord, and they said to Moses, 'Why did you bring us out here to die in the wilderness? Weren't there enough graves for us in Egypt? What have you done to us? Why did you make us leave Egypt? Didn't we tell you this would happen while we were still in Egypt? We said, "Leave us alone! Let us be slaves to the Egyptians. It's better to be a slave in Egypt than a corpse in the wilderness!"'

But Moses told the people, 'Don't be afraid. Just stand still and watch the Lord rescue you today. The Egyptians you see today will never be seen again. The Lord himself will fight for you. Just stay calm.'"

Sage advice from Moses, who faced the same situation as the people he was leading. God opened a path for them to cross the sea on dry ground. God made a way for them. Courage pushed them forward. All that was required was to stand still and watch the Lord work. Stand still and know that He is God (Psalm 46:10).

Prayer: *God, thank You for opening a path for me today. I pray that I can move forward courageously even when I am feeling fearful. I am comforted knowing that You are with me and opening a path for me.*

John 16:33 (NLT)

"I have told you all this so that you may have peace in me. Here on earth you will have many trials and sorrows. But take heart, because I have overcome the world."

Question: What will you choose today—courage or fear? Consider choosing courage.

VICTORY

During the fall season, I enjoy watching college football. The ups and downs throughout the game are exciting. The pursuit to get the ball into the end zone, the penalties, sacks, opposition, defense, third-down conversions, touchdowns, and career-long field goals hold my attention. I am thrilled when the university I attended heads to the conference championship game. Even when my boys played travel baseball, I witnessed many hard-fought tournament games that ended in our team winning. The exhilaration for the boys was inspiring.

Two teams prepare mentally and physically for months to arrive at the big game. They are prepared to execute every play. Both teams have a heart to win for themselves and their fans. The reality is, one team will lose, and one team will be victorious. Defeat is not easy.

As believers in Christ, we are on a team where we are eternally victorious. We possess victory. It doesn't even require a ton of effort. Christ our Lord did the heavy lifting when He was crucified on a cross, buried in a borrowed grave, and rose triumphantly. Living a life of victory is not a feeling but a declared state of being for a Christian. The world will tell us we are victims because of our past experiences. God proclaims we are victorious. Victory is defeating an opponent or enemy.

I Corinthians 15:57–58 (ESV)

"But thanks be to God, who gives us the victory through our Lord Jesus Christ.

Therefore, my beloved brothers, be steadfast, immovable, always abounding in the work of the Lord, knowing that in the Lord your labor is not in vain."

Look at the gift that was given to us. We have the gift of victory through our Lord Jesus Christ. It's not based on a set of circumstances or a certain privileged childhood. God said it. I believe it. We can be anchored, firmly planted, and confident because of this truth. Our adversary, Satan, will try to distract us from our position of victory.

The universal sign of victory is a raised chest, arms outstretched, fist pumped in the air, and a grin on your face. This gesture is innate and spontaneous. Whether you are an Olympic runner or clinching a conference championship, you will see the gesture of victory. That gesture is also a sign of dominance.

In Genesis 1:26, God declares we are made in His image, and we will have dominion over every living thing. We are winners in Christ Jesus. Today might be a sad day. It could also be a day when self-defeating thoughts and fear are screaming at you. Fear makes our world smaller because we are too afraid to move forward. God says you are victorious. I've had days when I am confused because the global world appears so dark and grim. God says we are victorious. If you are disoriented by grief, God declares you are victorious.

Prayer: *God, thank You that through Your son, Jesus Christ, I am victorious. In places where I am doubting or wavering, remind me of my position in You. I am a winner. Amen!*

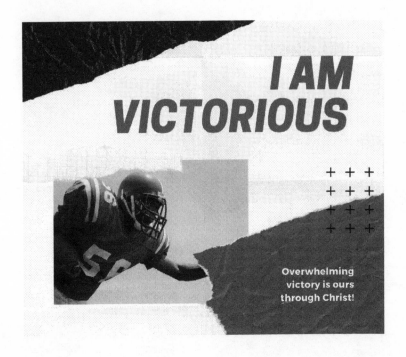

Romans 8:37 (NLT)

"No, despite all these things, overwhelming victory is ours through Christ, who loved us."

Question: What new aspects did you learn about being victorious?

PROCESS

I've spent many hours in a hair salon waiting on a process to finish. Every piece of the hair salon experience is designed for you to wait—wait to be called back for your appointment; wait for your hair color to process; wait for the relaxer to straighten your hair. Even the styling process takes time. I've tried many times to skip steps or rush through it. My hairstylist will always say, you will not get the results you desire by skipping steps. I do not like to wait.

Parenting is also a process of waiting. The larger my baby bump, the greater my expectancy towards the delivery date. I truly wanted to omit a few weeks at the end of the pregnancy. As mothers we want our babies to crawl, walk, eat solids, talk, get potty trained, learn to drive, and graduate. Why was I always in a rush? The world whizzes by, and you expect that instant gratification in every situation. Maybe you can identify.

There are seasons of life that are a grueling process. As we travel through a process, it takes time. The process of healing from surgery. Receiving a medical diagnosis is a process. The diagnosis is only the beginning of waiting. The remaining days are an upside down, inside out roller coaster ride. It's filled with lab work, PET scans, MRIs, radiation, evaluations, chemo, needles, etc. Waiting is not easy.

Psalm 27:14 (NLT)

"Wait patiently for the Lord. Be brave and courageous. Yes, wait patiently for the Lord."

The prophet Isaiah foretold of Jesus centuries before Jesus was born (Isaiah 9:6). Imagine eagerly waiting for the Messiah to arrive. Time passes, and no Messiah is in sight. Numerous spiritual giants waited. Abraham waited for his promised son to be born. Joseph waited through years of imprisonment, abundance, and famine. Esther waited until the right moment to make a request to King Xerxes.

A process can move slowly because it is a series of actions or steps for an achieved end. The process will appear to grind to a halt when we start comparing our process with that of others. I remember a period of unemployment. It seemed that everyone was receiving job offers except me. I was frustrated. I felt stuck. The more I gazed at others, the more I felt defeated.

The good news is God meets us in the process. He doesn't leave us. God is in everything. He orders every detail. Don't use today to worry about tomorrow.

God's process draws us into deeper intimacy. We are awakened to His presence. He teaches us lessons in our process. After we've suffered a little while, God promises to restore and strengthen us (I Peter 5:10). God will steady our feet on a firm foundation.

Prayer: *God, I acknowledge today that I have limited wisdom. This process seems scary and unending but I trust Your plan. I know that You have all the answers.*

Proverbs 3:6–7 (NLT)

"Seek his will in all you do, and he will show you which path to take. Don't be impressed with your own wisdom. Instead, fear the Lord and turn away from evil."

Question: What lessons are you learning during this process? This process has purpose.

AFFECTION

There are times I get in the mood to declutter parts of my house. I recently was in that type of organizing mood. I found an old tattered journal that I kept as a teenager. There were not any deep spiritual thoughts in that journal, just entries about friends and boys. I enjoyed my boy crushes as a teenager. As you can imagine, when you are a teenager you easily confuse affection with love.

Affection is simply a fondness for someone or something. I think of it as a strong like. One of my boy crushes over time blossomed into love. He is now my husband. As we go through life, we want to experience God's peace. We have a personal responsibility to grow in the knowledge of God. This strengthens our faith.

Our world is filled with many interruptions. We can miss the opportunity to grow and evolve. It's so easy to become complacent, especially when you daily fall into the same routine. An interruption leads us to miss our quiet time. Then that one day turns into weeks. When we move away from hearing God's voice daily, it ushers us down a path of misguided affections. The closer we move to God, the further we move away from Satan and his destructive voice.

We slowly start elevating what we know from the world's perspective. Our humanity needs to be reminded of how God is in complete control. He's the captain of our ship. God is faithful and pure in His ways. That assurance comes through studying His word.

Exodus 20:5 (NLT)

"You must not bow down to them or worship them, for I, the Lord your God, am a jealous God who will not tolerate your affection for any other gods...."

God is clear in His word, there should not be any other gods that take away our affection. We can elevate anything above God, like our affection for a car, sports team, pursuit of money, pursuit of perfection, pursuit of a perfect family. A child, relationship, business endeavor, job, or even ministry can all spiral to an idol status in our life.

God will not share His affection with anyone or anything. The transition from affection to love happens subtly. Before we know it, that which we had control over can control us. For instance, you pay off a credit card, and soon it's maxed out again. Strongholds take years to develop. It's a short slope from good intentions into a pit. For instance, it starts with someone giving you a simple compliment. As you continue to hear the same compliments, you begin to take the credit. God's glory becomes your own. Discreetly, seeds of pride are planted. Then those seeds are watered and sprout in unhealthy ways.

Prayer: *God, please remove anything that distracts me from seeing the power of Your glory manifested today. I don't want to be distracted* *from experiencing Your presence or hearing Your voice. I reserve my worship for You and not for items in my life. Show me where I have misguided affections or strongholds that need to be torn down.*

Psalm 51:10 (NIV)

"Create in me a pure heart, O God, and renew a steadfast spirit within me."

Question: What or who has gained idol status in your life?

RELEASE

⸻

Life quickly becomes routine. The mundane is familiar. During the pandemic, wearing masks was a new phenomenon. It quickly became the normal way of life to shop or interact with others. Toxic relationships or situations can initially start as dysfunctional and evolve into normal. The dysfunctional normal catapults to "just the way things are." How do you go from toxic and dysfunctional into normal so abruptly?

The ability to say no can become one of the most powerful words in our vocabulary. It's the ability to edit in our lives that can save our life. The most tedious part of writing a manuscript, being a photographer, producing a film, or preparing a speech is the editing process. When most people face a new year, they make resolutions or set goals. Those goals might require fewer tasks, less food intake, or less overscheduling. We desire to release the old and embrace the new. Disappointingly, many will bring the toxic and dysfunctional actions of last year into the new year.

There isn't a magic pill or drink that helps someone lose weight or shake off an addiction. It requires a release of old habits and thinking. It starts with a choice to say no, to turn down the old familiar ways. If we are honest with ourselves, we know there are things or people in our lives that do not serve us well. How do we release their control or influence over us? It starts with a choice of release, a commitment to release those places that hold us back and weigh us down. Don't sweat the small stuff.

Hebrews 12:1 (NLT)

"Therefore, since we are surrounded by such a huge crowd of witnesses to the life of faith, let us strip off every weight that slows us down, especially the sin that so easily hinders our progress. And let us run with endurance the race that God has set before us."

To release ourselves of unnecessary burdens, we must lay aside stress and worry, which very easily attaches itself to us. The ability to worry requires less effort than the ability to surrender. Worry is a learned behavior. It's a part of our DNA. With worry guiding us we want to figure it out, control the situation or narrative. Surrender can look like weakness. It appears as if we are just giving up. We aren't giving up, we are releasing it to God, simply because God is able to handle every detail.

As an active exercise enthusiast, I can tell when I've had too many carbohydrates or gained extra pounds. They slow me down. I don't pick up speed on my runs. I exercise at a slower pace. Extra fat in life situations or relationships can become a weight that drags on us. People can wear us down. Our energy is sucked out of us.

Envision a runner attempting to race with a backpack of dumbbell weights. They will move forward, but not at a reasonable pace. We must release the extra fat to experience the fullness of abundant living. Surrender the self-defeating and pessimistic thoughts. Release the procrastination and criticism of others and yourself. Remember, it all starts with a choice.

Prayer: *God, please reveal the areas in my life where I am not being served well. I want to release the relationships, situations, mindsets, or things that are weighing me down. I desire to run the race of life efficiently. I want to gaze at Your strength and stop trying to control those areas that are not controllable. Because You are my shepherd, I have all that I need today (Psalm 23:1).*

Psalm 55:22 (NLT)

"Give your burdens to the Lord, and he will take care of you. He will not permit the godly to slip and fall."

Questions: Are you feeling fainthearted? Are you feeling weary? What aspect of your life is not serving you well? Could this be an area for you to release and surrender at the foot of the cross? Because of who God is, you have everything you need.

TRUST

As a young mom, I trusted my intuition. When the boys would cry, for the most part I knew what they needed. In most cases, it was either a clean diaper, food, or a nap. Of course, there were times when I didn't know why they were crying. The long nights with the boys cutting teeth or being sick with ear infections was tough. I trust that doctors will give an accurate diagnosis. During the pandemic, I trusted the efficacy of wearing masks properly, social distancing, and handwashing. When I graduated from the University of Florida, I trusted that I would have a rock star job with a full compensation package once I graduated.

Even as I write this, I trust that technology operates properly for me to write and create. There are many ways we trust God with minimal effort. We trust that when we need things to work, they will operate properly: the chairs we sit in; our cars; high-speed internet to livestream our favorite programs.

During the sticky and tough times of life or the times when we need to make life-changing decisions, we must follow God's plan in regard to trust. Even when we do not know what to do next, we must trust He has a plan for us. We can't rely on feelings. Trusting feelings sends us down a path of wrong decision-making.

Proverbs 3:5 (NIV)

"Trust in the Lord with all your heart and lean not on your own understanding."

We are encouraged to trust God with all of our heart. Trust is a firm belief. Trust allows you to see a vision that isn't evident yet. God wants us to radically trust in Him. We can't trust our logic and reasoning. We must acknowledge our dependence on God. We put our confidence in God who is strong, powerful, mighty, and has no rival. God concentrates on us constantly. That is His providential care. We are cherished and valued by Him.

Since we live at a constant intersection of grace and grief, struggle and success, fear and faith, celebration and confusion, trusting can be challenging. We experience the best and worst of times simultaneously. God's plan never fails. We can trust in His ability to give us the strength we need today. His plan has always been loving and faithful.

Even when agony enveloped Jesus over His pending crucifixion, Jesus trusted the plan of His Heavenly Father. It was the type of agony that made sweat appear like drops of blood on His forehead. Jesus, completely consumed by anguish, still trusted the full plan of God (Luke 22:42–44). We will have moments of agony and discomfort just as Jesus did. That doesn't mean we are without faith. Tony Evans stated, "We can question God without questioning God." When wisdom is lacking, ask God to provide it. Trust how God replies to your prayer. Be open to hear His voice. Be willing to walk in obedience. Trust and obey. Walk together.

Prayer: *Lord, give me the freedom today to trust Your plan. I surrender my heart that wants to control and fast-track my character development. I trust that in all that I encounter today I will be given enough provision to carry me through it. Thank You that Your plan is trustworthy. Great is Your faithfulness.*

James 1:5 (NIV)

"If any of you lacks wisdom, you should ask God, who gives generously to all without finding fault, and it will be given to you."

Question: Where are you struggling today to trust God's plan?

Write it down, cross it out, and say, "God can handle it. I trust His plan."

ANCHOR

⌒

Early in childhood, I developed a love for words. I would compete in oratorical contests, which always scared me. But with each poem recited, I could see the power of words on full display. Many of the poems were written centuries ago, yet the impact of the words was surprisingly relevant for each audience. Words can uplift or words can destroy. Words can bring life or death into any situation. Words can bring joy. Words matter. Words have power.

In the most difficult times of my life and my immediate family's life, I've seen where the promises in scripture become a solid anchor. When my identical twin sister faced her cancer journey, she was captivated by God's words of healing. She would wake up listening to the Bible app. She would take morning walks praying. She would recite God's word during lunch. She would fall asleep with the Bible on her chest. She buried herself in a new way, reading scriptures that dealt with healing. Walking through dark days of adversity, our souls can drift afloat with worry. Through the word of God, we are anchored. Any pet owner who walks their dog on a leash knows that pup can only go so far. They take off after the squirrel only to realize they are tethered to their owner.

God provides hope: hope and assurance that God will be with us forever; hope that God will supply all our needs, not just physically, but also spiritually; hope that God's grace is sufficient to carry us securely through any storm or success. The anchor of hope is something I can hold onto. It tethers me to Christ. Hope grabs me.

I was recently taking an afternoon walk with my husband on a hot summer afternoon. The humidity was so thick it stuck to you. We heard a horrible noise coming from the tree. We looked up to find two squirrels fighting. These squirrels were so unaware of us they fell in front of us, scaring me horribly. My husband grabbed me to keep me from running into the fire hydrant. I am thankful that he was an anchor of support. Isn't it natural that when we feel ourselves falling, we look for something to grab onto?

During times when life seems out of control, we crave the ability to hold onto something. We need an anchor. Christ is our anchor. He is able to keep, lead, love, and protect us.

Philippians 4:11–13 (NIV)

"I am not saying this because I am in need, for I have learned to be content whatever the circumstances. I know what it is to be in need, and I know what it is to have plenty. I have learned the secret of being content in any and every situation, whether well fed or hungry, whether living in plenty or in want. I can do all this through him who gives me strength."

Prayer: *God, help me have clarity today that You are my anchor. I don't need to look to the world to solve and satisfy life challenges. I am trusting You today for my hope, peace, and joy. I know that in each of these experiences, I am growing stronger.*

Hebrews 11:1 (NLT)

"What is faith? It is the confident assurance that what we hope for is going to happen. It is the evidence of things we cannot yet see."

Question: Where do you anchor yourself during tough times?

EQUIPPED

⟋‿⟍

Icried during my youngest son's graduation from Pre-K. I am a sucker for those types of moments. I couldn't believe time passed so swiftly and he was moving into kindergarten. Graduation is an exciting yet challenging time. All new friends and experiences lie ahead. It's a rite of passage that the student is moving into a level of higher responsibility. It's a new chapter.

My boys handled the first day of kindergarten better than I did. They walked right into the school with zero fear. I, on the other hand, went to the boo-hoo breakfast in the school's cafeteria. It felt comforting to be surrounded by other parents nursing the same emotions as I was. Our kids can move forward because they are resilient and equipped. Behind those tears was anxiety about how the boys would handle the school setting. I wondered if they would miss me. Clearly, they didn't.

David, in the Bible, was a young king. He was overlooked because of his age. We don't want to assume who is best for an assignment in our life based on appearance. That leads to wrong judgments about people. David's spirit was one of confidence and boldness despite being the youngest. Even though he was fighting a giant stronger and older than he was, he didn't back down from the challenge. He felt equipped for the battle. David was courageous. He knew his strength came from God.

He was given armor to fight the giant Goliath. David decided to use different weapons. He didn't rely on the familiarity and logistics of the military. He possessed a Godly wisdom that was more precious than common battle strategies.

I Samuel 17:45–47 (NLT)

"David replied to the Philistine, 'You come to me with sword, spear, and javelin, but I come to you in the name of the Lord of Heaven's Armies—the God of the armies of Israel, whom you have defied. Today the Lord will conquer you, and I will kill you and cut off your head. And then I will give the dead bodies of your men to the birds and wild animals, and the whole world will know that there is a God in Israel! And everyone assembled here will know that the Lord rescues his people, but not with sword and spear. This is the Lord's battle, and he will give you to us!'"

David was equipped for this fight. He spoke with authority, assurance, and confidence. His preparation in the fields fighting lions and bears would allow him to defeat Goliath. You are prepared and equipped for every calamity or success that comes to you. We face many different giants in life. Just like my son walking into that school, you will rise to the occasion to defeat the giant in front of you.

Prayer: *I am equipped for this fight. Today, I will walk with boldness and fearlessness. Every obstacle is defeated. Because of God, I have overwhelming victory. (Romans 8:37)*

Hebrews 13:21 (NLT)

"May he equip you with all you need for doing his will. May he produce in you, through the power of Jesus Christ, every good thing that is pleasing to him. All glory to him forever and ever! Amen."

Question: What strength do you possess that equips you today for challenges you are facing?

PREPARED

I ran a half marathon years ago, and that was a tough challenge. There was so much anticipation when I trained for the race. The Florida humidity sucks the life out of you during training. I would be drenched when I returned home. I spent time on the weekends completing a long run to be prepared for the race.

I vividly remember reaching mile eleven on race day and realized I couldn't breathe. Literally, it felt as if my lungs stopped working. I barely completed the race. I was so confused about what was happening inside my body. I was running that race with my sister. I told her I was in distress, but she laughed it off and told me I was just tired. No help there.

Thankfully, I slowed down and eventually fell across the finish line. I immediately went to the medical tent. Sure enough, air was not passing freely through my lungs. I was diagnosed with exercise-induced asthma. I've never experienced that before. That day, my mind was ready to run the race but my lungs were not prepared. During my training, my run buddy would provide me a scripture of inspiration.

I Corinthians 9:25–26 (NLT)

"All athletes are disciplined in their training. They do it to win a prize that will fade away, but we do it for an eternal prize. So I run with purpose in every step…"

Preparation gets us ready for the crisis. We do not want to wait until the battle starts to begin preparing. The daily preparation of praying, studying scripture, being still, having faith, and meditation prepares us for the unknown moments of life. If we aren't making a plan, we are planning to fail.

Remember how you felt before your first date? You prepared what you would wear, where you would go, what movie to watch, etc. God wants us in a state of preparedness. Living in South Florida, we know that tropical storms come out of nowhere. Before hurricane season starts, we are told to prepare our homes for any possibility of storms. Waiting until the last minute to prepare causes anxiety. Preparation saves money and time. Noah built an ark before there was rain. It was built in preparation of the forecasted torrential flooding.

Distractions will come to take us away from preparation. It reminds me of college and seeing the deadlines on the syllabus at the beginning of the semester. I always thought I had so much time for the large projects and papers due at the end of the class. Distractions came, and I would always scramble. It never failed. I would wait until the last minute, resulting in many late nights to finish. Has that ever happened to you— procrastination? Distractions, such as social media, can zap our time and drift us away. What are your time wasters? God will give us the instructions needed to weather any storm or situation. We must prepare to hear the instructions. We want to be in a position to discern His voice. Let's keep our focus fixed on His truths.

Prayer: *Today I commit to spending time with You, Lord. I don't want the distractions of the day to pull me away from hearing Your voice. I am running towards my heavenly reward, and that takes prayer, scripture study, fasting, intimacy with You, and worship.*

Exodus 19:10 (NLT)

"Then the Lord told Moses, 'Go down and prepare the people for my arrival. Consecrate them today and tomorrow, and have them wash their clothing.'"

Questions: What is a time waster in your schedule today? What tasks can be edited from your calendar? Time spent with God moves us further from hearing the wrong voices.

SHAKEN

There has been a wave of silence across our global world. During the pandemic of 2020, the first sound of the virus was silence as the world shut down. It was a global pause and reset—something most people never experienced. Finances, work, school, shopping all came screeching to a halt. It looked like every system intertwined in our society was failing. Food shortages and fragile supply chains added to the silence.

In full transparency, I was anxious, shocked, discouraged, and afraid—completely rocked to my core. As a parent, you quickly have to evaluate situations and then try to explain them to your kids. It's hard to explain an audible shaking that took over our world. Thankfully, feeling fear does not mean our faith is failing. You can have faith and experience fear all at the same time. It means that we are human.

There are many instances in scripture when God delivers a message and He starts by saying, "Do not be afraid." (Luke 1:30) God would speak this statement because people were afraid. The most prolific personalities in scripture felt afraid. Life is scary. Feelings are not facts. They fluctuate constantly. We can attempt to stuff down our feelings, but feelings will eat us alive. Suppressing a feeling brings it back stronger. Buried feelings re-emerge. The book of Psalms is full of humans navigating a myriad of emotions. You read about those that spent time praising and those that felt disdain.

Psalm 16:8 (NLT)

"I know the Lord is always with me. I will not be shaken, for he is right beside me."

We might not always feel that God is beside us, but He is. As negative feelings come, focus your mind back to the truth of God's word. God is with you. Sitting in the seat of uncertainty is scary. Times spent in seasons of struggle and sorrow are unwelcomed. Seasons of sorrow are like winter. You can't control the timing; it just arrives. Winter is a harsh and dark season. Sorrow either shapes or shakes our faith. We are pressed, but in that process we are growing. It's like the demo day for a new kitchen remodel. Completely gut it to build it back better.

Recite the truth of God's word constantly. Say it out loud so that it interrupts any negative thoughts. Reciting a verse multiple times a day allows it to slowly penetrate our heart. When the ground beneath us is shaking, we remain anchored by God's truth.

Psalm 37:23 (NLT)

"The Lord directs the steps of the godly. He delights in every detail of their lives."

Prayer: *God is great. God is mighty. God is powerful. God is love. This is the prayer of my heart today. I won't be shaken by the events of today because my trust is in You, oh Lord.*

Numbers 6:24–26 (NLT)

"May the Lord bless you and protect you. May the Lord smile on you and be gracious to you. May the Lord show you his favor and give you his peace."

Question: Are you experiencing a shake-up in your world today? Remind yourself of God's love for you.

FASTEN

───⌒───

Visiting the doctor isn't always pleasant. I ensured my boys met all of their milestone appointments. However, once you enter adulthood, you slack off a bit with your own annual physicals. The body will send gentle whispers to slow down or eat less. You ignore them until your body screams at you. That happened to me. I was experiencing random heart palpitations. I attributed this to my breathless schedule that included a full travel schedule, work, community commitments, and parenting.

My doctor wasn't pleased that I'd waited to visit. When I scheduled the appointment, I thought I had been in the office eighteen months ago. It was actually four years since I'd visited the doctor. Putting others as a priority will catch up to you. You can't pour from an empty cup. It's important to take care of our own health first. After some exploratory tests, observation, and a diagnosis, I received a prescription. It wasn't just medicine but some lifestyle changes that I needed to make immediately. This included taking an evening walk to decompress from work.

I was giving myself away, and it wasn't healthy. I wasn't focusing on my health. If I had been, I would have seen the warning signs. Physical health and mental health are fragile. They require careful nurturing. We must be mindful of what we are thinking. The battle for our mental health starts in our minds and eventually affects our behaviors. A spark of negative thinking can grow into an inferno of wrong decisions.

Philippians 4:8 (NLT)

"And now, dear brothers and sisters, one final thing. Fix your thoughts on what is true, and honorable, and right, and pure, and lovely, and admirable. Think about things that are excellent and worthy of praise."

Fasten thoughts around ideas that are positive and truthful. Fasten thoughts on God's glorious work. Fasten thoughts on all of God's benefits (Psalm 103). This takes practice. We must be intentional with our thought life. Tethering to God's truths is invaluable.

We can focus on blessings versus what is lost. There is a battle for peace in our mind. Keep your mind fastened on God's strength. Scripture becomes a prescription that heals and soothes. Choose to form new habits.

Every news headline or notification is enough to cause us to panic. Limiting distractions can work wonders for mental health. It is easy to follow the behaviors of this world. The external culture frames our sense of self. We can become calcified in our thinking. That impacts the way we think, act, and speak. If we are stuck in patterns that don't serve us well, remove them. This sometimes requires us to edit certain relationships out of our life. Toxic people drain us of vital energy we need.

Prayer: *I am fastening my thoughts on what is true, honorable, right, and admirable. I want to fix my thoughts on things that are excellent and worthy of praise. I will fill myself today with Your truths.*

Romans 12:2 (NLT)

"Don't copy the behavior and customs of this world, but let God transform you into a new person by changing the way you think. Then you will learn to know God's will for you, which is good and pleasing and perfect."

Question: What biblical truth will you fasten to today?

ACTION

I remember a time when there was an urgent request for people to step up during the 2020 general election. There was a risk of not having enough poll workers. My heart was pricked. I was nudged to solve a problem. Voting is a right of citizens who live in a democracy. I was out of my comfort zone on that election day, but remembered the call to action I felt initially.

I'd complained and was frustrated on previous election nights. Many times, after a general election, I saw my county on the national news due to election mishaps. Instead of complaining, God led me to act. It gave me an opportunity to understand the process I once criticized. I had a God assignment.

We can spend time complaining about a situation, but that does not solve the problem. Bitterness doesn't lead to solutions. Nehemiah, in the Bible, was a problem solver. He saw his ancestral home lying in ruins. He set out to rebuild a wall that provided security for his nation. While he was there, he saw the poorest citizens being taken advantage of. They were working yet still in debt. They were selling their kids into slavery to pay those debts. Nehemiah's heart was spurred to action. Nehemiah understood that complaining didn't advance the Kingdom of God's agenda.

Nehemiah stayed on the wall through opposition and rejection. He was relentless in continuing to work in the assignment God gave him. As he worked and witnessed a societal injustice, he spoke up. He was moved to action. Nehemiah was on the wall, building. He could have dismissed the public outcry. Nehemiah purposely chose to address it versus being apathetic to it.

Nehemiah 5:9–11 (NIV)

"So I continued, 'What you are doing is not right. Shouldn't you walk in the fear of our God to avoid the reproach of our Gentile enemies? I and my brothers and my men are also lending the people money and grain. But let us stop charging interest! Give back to them immediately their fields, vineyards, olive groves and houses, and also the interest you are charging them—one percent of the money, grain, new wine and olive oil.'"

Nehemiah's anger was channeled to action. His heart was pricked. When we are angry, we can pause, pray, ponder and position ourselves to hear God. We want to hear His voice before we take action. Caring requires action. Taking action requires hard work. It requires focus, tenacity, and grit. We can sit quietly and have an idea. Often because of distractions it becomes a fleeting thought, whizzing by never to be remembered. I want to be inspired to implement the God idea. Stay on the wall like Nehemiah to accomplish the God assignments in your life.

Prayer: *God, will You awaken us to the injustices in our lives. Show us any offensive way we have mistreated someone. God, I pray for* *justice, fairness, and equality in our global world. As an image bearer (Genesis 1:26) I want to be moved to action. Through my actions today, may the light of You shine bright in our world.*

Matthew 14:16 (NLT)

"But Jesus replied, 'That isn't necessary—you feed them.'"

Questions: Where will you take action today? Is there anywhere you can channel anger into positive action?

CONFIDENCE

⁓

As a young girl, I was afraid to speak in public. My mom would have us compete in an oratorical contest or volunteer during youth services on Sunday to read scripture. I didn't like it. I did not have much confidence in myself or my speaking ability. I was frightened, and my stomach would be in knots before I would speak. I had no idea at the time that God was preparing me.

Moses had a similar experience in the Bible when he was in front of the burning bush that wasn't being consumed by the fire. He removed his shoes because the ground was declared holy. He was commanded to tell the king Pharaoh to let the children of Israel go from a life of slavery and oppression. Moses wasn't comfortable in his speaking abilities. Moses was before God, yet he was focusing on his limitations.

Exodus 4:10 (NLT)

"But Moses pleaded with the Lord, 'O Lord, I'm not very good with words. I never have been, and I'm not now, even though you have spoken to me. I get tongue-tied, and my words get tangled.'"

It is easy to focus on our weaknesses when God makes a request. God prepares us even during our childhood for our life purpose and assignments. Each experience we encounter prepares us and builds confidence in our ability to trust Him. I learned at an early age how to have confidence in God when I felt out of my realm to perform.

Confidence is trust on steroids. Confidence is defined as a firm trust, one where you aren't wavering or doubting. It means you can rely fully on God and have confidence in Him. Psalm 146:3 instructs us not to put our confidence in powerful people; there is no hope for you there. Our confidence takes time to be developed and established. We can have confidence in God.

Prayer: *Lord, I declare that my firm trust is in God. I thank You for the seasons of preparation even when they are uncomfortable. Thank You for the experiences that will happen today. Help me place my anchor in You and not people.*

Hebrews 4:15-16 (NIV)

"For we do not have a high priest who is unable to empathize with our weaknesses, but we have one who has been tempted in every way, just as we are—yet he did not sin. Let us then approach God's throne of grace with confidence, so that we may receive mercy and find grace to help us in our time of need."

Question: Have you ever been stretched to the point of discomfort? God might be preparing you for something greater. Remain confident in Christ. Your life matters and has value.

HARMONY

⌒

There are days when it feels that I lose track of time. No matter how many emails I read there are always more. I complete one project and another one is added to my task list. I've learned the hard way that being busy doesn't equate to being productive. We all have the same 168 hours every week. About three years ago, I kept a time log for one week. I wanted to see exactly how my time was evaporating. Tracking my time became instrumental in finding areas of waste. I started reading books to replace the pockets of time where I would normally watch TV. I started creating margin in my schedule to remove the feeling of always running breathlessly to the next appointment. I made decisive choices on how I wanted to use that blank slate of 168 hours every week.

I long to aim for harmony in my life. In my head, I imagine an orchestra with many different instruments and sections. They all come together in synergy to produce an incredible sound. I want my life to come together in concert. How do I find harmony, not just in my own life, but also when I interact with others?

Harmony doesn't mean we agree all the time with someone. A married couple can have a harmonious relationship and still have passionate disagreements. The God-type harmony builds each of us up individually so that we can come together focused on and operating towards a common goal. It is precious and pleasant when we can live together in harmony (Psalm 133:1). Colossians 3:12–14 shows that we will have to clothe ourselves in tender-hearted mercy, kindness, humility, gentleness, and patience.

The world we see is full of strife, division, and chaos. We will have different ideas than other people. Diversity of thought is needed to make stronger decisions. It's the different ideas, experiences, and cultural backgrounds that can cause conflict. It naturally happens when two or more people are together. The friction is different ideas bumping up against each other. We will experience greater innovation and new ideas when we approach our world with a spirit of harmony.

To arrive at harmony, we will have to make allowance for our faults and others' faults. We will be required to forgive the way Christ forgave us. Forgive, not forget. When we lead with love, we will find it easier to achieve harmony and find that common ground.

Romans 15:5 (NLT)

"May God, who gives this patience and encouragement, help you live in complete harmony with each other, as is fitting for followers of Christ Jesus."

Prayer: *Lord, I commit to lead with love today. I know I might encounter a person or situation that is unsettling and uncertain. I will bring love into my day so that I might achieve the harmony of working toward the common goal of loving God and loving others.*

Psalm 133:1 (NLT)

"How wonderful and pleasant it is when brothers live together in harmony!"

Question: What outward expression will represent harmony in your relationships?

PEACE

Speaking the word peace brings comfort. Peace is a universal symbol of the type of relationships we want in our world. Government and foreign leaders collaborate with allies and adversaries to achieve peace relations. When you navigate through what has been described as "the toughest year this century," you search for peace in numerous places. Peace can feel like an aspirational destination, something that we might not ever attain.

Peace shows up in different ways. It can be a comforting word from a friend, pastor, or mentor. It also appears while someone is listening to a song. God is light. Realizing that God knows the path ahead can bring peace. God reveals His plan.

Psalm 27:1

"The Lord is my light and my salvation—so why should I be afraid? The Lord is my fortress, protecting me from danger, so why should I tremble?"

The author of this psalm was David. He was secretly anointed as king. He was tasked at a young age with leading a nation. It was a seat of uncertainty. David was a man after God's heart.

Security is not found in the government, occupation, or a profitable bank account. Peace and security come from God. When the details of life are sketchy, God has made a way.

I went through a season of wanting to amass wealth. You feel more financially secure having money in a bank account. Honestly, who doesn't want more money? Money gives you more options. You can buy stuff with money. The boys played with a toy cash register and never wanted to share their "monies" as young children. They would cringe every time they would have to spend their allotted cash in the game Monopoly Empire.

Money is not the currency of heaven. God can provide wisdom that carries more value than money—wisdom to make a wise and prudent decision. God downloads strategies, inventions, and ideas that catapult people into national prominence—innovation that solves some of the world's most complex problems. Stop looking for God to show up in the limited way you envision. It distracts you from seeing how God is already providing.

There are days when fear will loom over us. David asks a poignant question: Why should I be afraid? Ask yourself that question. Why should you be afraid? The grind and busyness of daily living can lull us into a false sense of security. God wants us to have peace in the provision He provides. The world paints a different picture on how to attain peace. Graduating from college, having a high credit score, amassing a large retirement fund, and buying a luxury car or a house are a few examples.

David decided that true peace came from being in the presence of God. The thing he sought most was dwelling in the house of the Lord. Peace enveloped David while he meditated on God's goodness (Psalm 27:4). Peace is not provided by a well-stocked food pantry. God offers peace that passeth all understanding, even when we are living on less—the type of peace that meets you during seasons of suffering. It meets you during winter seasons when life feels harsher. We all have a different measure of what our winter season looks like, but we've experienced it. God left this peace for us; it was a gift (John 14:27). Will you receive that gift today? It starts with a deliberate choice. You will have peace. Open God's gift of peace. Peace comforts a heart that is troubled.

Prayer: *God, today I thank You for peace. The precious gift of peace is beyond my ability to comprehend. My heart is restless, but I rest in Your peace. Please carry me safely through this day. I want to experience Your peace. I praise You for guarding my heart today with peace.*

2 Thessalonians 3:16 (NLT)

"Now may the Lord of peace himself give you his peace at all times and in every situation. The Lord be with you all."

Questions: Are you confident in the peace God provides? What do you fear today?

RELAX

⟶

During my son's senior year in high school, I was frazzled and breathless. The ability to juggle work, home, community commitments and manage the details of senior year caused long nights and early mornings. I was trying to burn the candle at both ends. Every encounter with my son led to a list of questions about the completion of his to do list. I attempted to bring my son into my level of worry and stress. He would grab my shoulders and say, "Mom, relax!" I truly didn't understand how to physically, emotionally, or mentally relax that year. I needed to relax in all three areas. I found it easy to just lounge on the couch "relaxing," but my mind was racing with all the tasks that needed to be accomplished. That was not mental rest.

Jesus experiences a weather storm that encompasses not only Him but His disciples. They experience the exact same storm, on the same night, traveling in the same boat, yet they had very different responses.

Mark 4:36–39 (NLT)

"So they took Jesus in the boat and started out, leaving the crowds behind (although other boats followed). But soon a fierce storm came up. High waves were breaking into the boat, and it began to fill with water. Jesus was sleeping at the back of the boat with his head on a cushion. The disciples woke him up, shouting, 'Teacher, don't you care that we're going to drown?' When Jesus woke up, he rebuked the wind and said to the waves, **'Silence! Be still!'** Suddenly the wind stopped, and there was a great calm."

We can take a posture of relaxation during storms of life because of *who* is in the boat with us. Again, Jesus was in the same boat, experiencing the same storm, and He was asleep while the disciples were shouting and frantic. That senior year of my son's graduation, I was frantic. I didn't ask for help from anyone. I didn't delegate responsibility. I was plowing ahead burning myself out.

Today we can commit to relax in the everlasting arms of Jesus. We will relax in His authority over the storm, relax in His peace, and relax in His strength to conquer all. We are more than conquerors (Romans 8:37). We can recline and lean into His presence. We can open our word and become refreshed. We can sing the lyrics to a song that usher in serenity. We can unwind from trying to handle everything. No one can give God counsel. He knows all things. We can rejoice that we have the mind of Christ (I Corinthians 2:16) if we are a believer. Remembering who God is allows me to rest in Him.

Prayer: *Thank You, Jesus, that I can take a posture of resting in Your everlasting arms. I can relax in who You are and trust that You are in the boat with me. I am not alone. Your plan towards me is good. I am fearfully and wonderfully made in Your image. I choose today to be an image-bearer of Jesus Christ. In my quiet spaces (when no one is watching), I relax in You.*

Matthew 11:30 (NLT)

"For my yoke is easy to bear, and the burden I give you is light."

Question: Are you feeling weighed down today? Take a breath. Lean into the light of God's presence. God is with you. Remember who He is.

BUT

～⌒～

Have you ever felt that curveballs are coming from every direction? My oldest son was a pitcher for some travel baseball teams. We were proud when he got the opportunity to travel to Cooperstown Baseball World. This is a premier week-long tournament held in upstate New York. My son spent years training with a pitching coach.

My son had different pitches in his arsenal. He relied on throwing his fastball pitch. The pitches are thrown to get the opponent to strike out. At the young age of twelve, the curveball was the most dangerous pitch he learned. It was thrown at a slower speed. The batter expected a fastball. He used this pitch sparingly. His fastball would whizz by the batters so efficiently. A curveball pitch was designed to throw the opposing athlete off his game. The coach wanted him to throw that batter off balance. Life throws us curveballs.

Has the normal routine of life been interrupted? Does it feel that the enemy is working overtime? I think we all can identify with times where nothing seems to go right. Your life can also be interrupted by success. But the blessing of success can be overwhelming as you navigate a learning curve in a new role. In my own life I think of being a new parent.

There are many fiery curveballs that the enemy will throw our way. God has given us a specific line in the Heavenly Father's prayer to be armed. It says, "deliver me from the evil one." We were once in the enemy's camp before we accepted salvation from Christ. Ephesians 2:1–3 talks about our fate before Christ. Then in verse 4 it starts with one of my favorite words in scripture: *but*. But God who loves us and is rich in mercy made us alive with Christ.

The word but is a conjunction. When you see the word but, it alerts you that there will be a contrasting statement. Ephesians 2 starts off talking about darkness, disobedience, and living in a way that satisfied the cravings of our flesh. Then scripture takes a dramatic reversal. We were once dead, but now have been made alive by Christ. We sit with Him in heavenly realms. This is a but God moment.

Ephesians 2:4 (NLT)

"But God is so rich in mercy, and he loved us so very much."

Today might be a day when the enemy tries to throw a fiery dart, but God will not allow that dart against you to prosper. When Jesus faced the cross and crucifixion, He was filled with anguish. In Luke 22:42, Jesus asked for the bitter cup to be removed and then said, "Nevertheless, not my will, BUT yours, be done."

Prayer: *I wait with great expectation for the dramatic reversal in my life. As the fiery darts shoot towards me, I surrender to the perfect plan of God. Nothing stops the plan of God in my life. I feel anguish and sadness, but I put my trust in You, God.*

Isaiah 54:17 (KJV)

"No weapon that is formed against thee shall prosper; and every tongue that shall rise against thee in judgment thou shalt condemn...."

Question: What is the curveball in your life today? It's designed to slow you down and get you off balance. Stay alert and ready.

LOVE

On days filled with triumph and accomplishments, God loves us. On days that are normal, God loves us. His love for us is not based on our actions. On days filled with hardship and pain, God loves us. I know that is hard to believe because in the moment the pain feels so awful. On happy days, it is easier for us to admit that God loves us. On those tough days we think:

Does He love me?

Did God forget about me?

Is He still here?

Is He angry with me?

Is He punishing me?

In Romans, we are reminded that nothing separates us from the love of God.

Romans 8:38 (NLT)

"And I am convinced that nothing can ever separate us from God's love. Neither death nor life, neither angels nor demons, neither our fears for today nor our worries about tomorrow—not even the powers of hell can separate us from God's love."

Nothing takes away from the love God already has for you. Also, nothing adds to the love He has for you. The more work you do, or the more volunteering in ministry doesn't add more love to you. God's love is a perfect and unconditional love that is lavishly given to us. Our human minds can find this hard to imagine because we equate love with some type of performance. God's love overtakes us. Let's commit to open our eyes to the many ways that God is showing His love today.

When life is hard, tough, and prickly God loves you. We can't compare His love to the love we've had from earthly relationships. God's love is infinitely more wise, loving, fair, generous, just, and kinder than anything we will see on Earth. It is a perfect and sacrificial love. God pursues us with His love. He commands us in I John 4:7 to continue in His love. His love is a daily walk.

Romans 5:8 (NLT)

"But God showed his great love for us by sending Christ to die for us while we were still sinners."

Before we knew God, He knew us. He formed our bodies in utter darkness and seclusion. He declares that our bodies are fearfully and wonderfully made. Our world is craving the love of God. It's the love of God that should radiate into our world.

Love is louder than hate. God isn't absent. He is still here loving you.

Prayer: *God, I appreciate the love You give to me. It has paved a path for me to show love to others. I pray today that I walk in Your love, because You are love.*

I John 4:19 (NLT)

"We love each other as a result of his loving us first."

Questions: What is one way to demonstrate God's love today to someone else? What can you do today to intentionally remember God's love for you?

REVIVE

Do you remember the first day of school? I would barely sleep the night before the first day of school. I was excited to meet my new teachers and see my friends. I received new clothes, a backpack, lunchbox, and new school supplies. My mom was an educator so we were immensely prepared for the first day. Aside from Christmas, as a child the first day of school was one of the most anticipated days of the year.

A new school year, new teachers, maybe even a new school, all provided a fresh start. All new folders, paper, and supplies were nostalgic. All the yellow #2 pencils were sharpened. Summer ended. Meeting the teacher was successful. Clothes were ironed precisely and laid out for the first day. Now it was time to work hard and achieve goals. Everyone starts with an A and a blank slate on the first day. Teachers have a fresh energy after a long summer break. The decisions students make throughout the year either maintain or drop that A grade.

God uses situations in our lives to revive us or give us that fresh-start feeling like students on the first day of school. The mundane and routine make life too comfortable and boring. Every now and then we all need to be revived. We aren't just going through the motions of the day but feeling a restoration of passion, effort, and energy. Even in family relationships we need to be revived. It is easy to be stuck in a rut with our kids or in our marriages.

As we walk with God, there are times we need revival. It's a refreshing and restorative jumpstart. It's experiencing a fresh touch of God's love; falling in love with Him again; feeling the fire that led us into salvation. We can become comfortable in our distractions and drift. Ministry and serving become monotonous. For instance, becoming unemployed became a catalyst for me to be revived to find a new industry and new path forward. I was able to rekindle prior network connections.

Psalm 85:6–7 (NLT)

"Won't you revive us again, so your people can rejoice in you? Show us your unfailing love, O Lord, and grant us your salvation."

A new car or relationship can't spiritually revive us. We need God to refresh us. As we look around our world, we see chaos and crisis. It looks like defeat. When we trust God and His plan, defeat is only an illusion. God has an eternal plan for us to live abundantly. We are more than conquerors (Romans 8:37). Your situation is not lost; it's being revived. Starting is easy. The middle is messy. That's when we need to be revived. God is restoring you into a place of full faith in Him. He's drawing you closer.

Prayer: *God, I admit there are moments when I lose hope. I feel defeated and far away from You. Please revive my spirit. I know that with one word You can set a fire in my soul. Revival starts with repentance. Forgive me for not trusting or wavering with doubt. I commit to lean not to my own understanding, but to trust You in all Your ways.*

Genesis 45:27 (NLT)

"But when they had given him Joseph's messages, and when he saw the wagons loaded with the food sent by Joseph, his spirit revived."

Questions: Where do you need a revival in your life? How will you jumpstart a closer relationship with God?

FORGET

I regret the days when I forget where I put my readers. Without them, life up close is blurry. I slide them on, and life and the words on the page are crystal clear. Unfortunately, I've purchased several pairs of readers because I lay them down and don't remember where I placed them. Have you ever torn up your house looking for an item? Maybe it was keys, a cell phone, glasses, a dental retainer, or the TV remote.

When it comes to my phone or keys, I will panic. I feel confident that I know the last place I saw them. My blood pressure rises. My heart is pounding as I search for the missing item. I start sweating and sometimes blaming others for losing them. Happiness disappears when I am searching. I quickly become anxious and confused.

I imagine Mary felt this way the first Easter morning. She wanted to know where the missing body of Jesus (John 20) was placed. Where did they put Him? She was confident that He was laid in a tomb located in the garden.

Mary summons Peter and John. They both run to the tomb. I can envision them being out of breath as they confirm the body of Jesus is missing. This becomes a mystery to them. After the men leave, Mary lingers at the tomb, weeping.

John 20:14–15 (NKJV)

"Now when she had said this, she turned around and saw Jesus standing there, and did not know that it was Jesus. Jesus said to her, 'Woman, why are you weeping? Whom are you seeking?' She, supposing him to be the gardener, said to him, 'Sir, if you have carried him away, tell me where you have laid him, and I will take him away.'"

In the midst of all this emotion and the frazzled behavior of weeping, sadness, shock, confusion, grieving, fear, and doubt, they all forgot what Jesus told them. Jesus predicted His own death. He told His disciples that He would enter into His glory (John 12:23). He told them that sadness would be turned to joy. In a little while they would not see Him anymore. Then they would see Him again (John 16:16).

In the midst of heightened emotion, they forgot. In the midst of confusion and shock, they forgot. In the midst of weeping and sadness, they forgot. Humanity wavers through a plethora of emotions. But what are we forgetting that the Lord has already told us? What promises are forgotten?

He's promised to keep us in perfect peace. God will be with us always. He assures us that He's our refuge and strength (Psalm 46:1). He protects us (Psalm 91). When we rely on logic and our own understanding, we forget. During happy days or crises let us commit to remember what the Lord told us. In the midst of chaos may there also be clarity.

Prayer: *God, when I forget Your promise or Your truths, I panic. I am forgetful because life distracts me. Today I will walk in encouragement and look up to remember Your greatness.*

Luke 24:5–7 (NKJV)

"Then, as they were afraid and bowed their faces to the earth, they said to them, 'Why do you seek the living among the dead? He is not here, but is risen! Remember how he spoke to you when he was still in Galilee, saying, "The Son of Man must be delivered into the hands of sinful men, and be crucified, and the third day rise again." ' "

Question: What have you forgotten? Weeping turns to rejoicing when we remember.

ARMOR

⌒

God has built you stormproof. You are able to live through challenging times as well as times of success. Being stormproof requires you to keep your focus on God. Focus on God is a superpower. Tell those self-defeating and anxious thoughts to get away. You are living through this part of history for a reason. There is a God purpose attached to you.

Whenever we set forth to live out our God-given purpose, opposition will come. Don't be distracted by it. It's the enemy's way of making you second guess your calling. Fear comes to derail the plans God has for your life. That is why we put on the armor of God. It is a gift from God. The armor is not just for times of battle but also times of preparation. The battles we face are not against people. We are facing an inescapable enemy.

Ephesians 6:10–12 (NIV)

"Finally, be strong in the Lord and in his mighty power. Put on the full armor of God, so that you can take your stand against the devil's schemes. For our struggle is not against flesh and blood, but against the rulers, against the authorities, against the powers of this dark world and against the spiritual forces of evil in heavenly realms."

You are not putting on the armor to win a battle. We already have victory in Jesus. You are fighting to stand firmly and peacefully in the arms of God. We often try to stand in our own strength. This leads to exhaustion. We walk, move, and operate in life because of the finished work on the cross by Jesus Christ.

You do not have to fight to receive anything from the Lord. You just have to believe. Your readiness comes from wearing the full armor. Men and women on SWAT teams prepare constantly with training and wearing their tactical gear. We are stormproof and ready for action with the armor of God.

Prayer: *God, I remain a soldier in Your army, living out the purpose and assignment You've given me. In moments when I'm slipping from that purpose, remind me. I refuse to be distracted by opposition, self-defeating thoughts, and fear. I go forward today with Your strength.*

Isaiah 58:11 (NLT)

The Lord will guide you continually, giving you water when you are dry and restoring your strength. You will be like a well-watered garden, like an ever-flowing spring.

Questions: What is your God-given gift/purpose? Are you battle ready today?

You will be like a well-watered garden ~ Isaiah 58:11

CONTINUE

I've experienced scary moments as a parent. Staying in the hospital with both boys was frightful. When kids are in ER triage for an evaluation, it's shocking. I didn't know what was medically wrong. I just knew my son was in distress with labored breathing. There wasn't time to pray since the room was spinning and time was moving quickly. During one trip, they didn't even register him. They whisked him away and immediately started working on his tiny body. He was in urgent need of a medical professional.

There is a part of me that thinks I can store up prayers for moments like that. A prayer cloud would be a great invention. A prayer is simply communication with God. With every whisper, shout, cry, or groan, I feel His presence. I want to walk in deliberate dependence on Him. When I do, I am at rest mentally.

A simple prayer shifted my focus from the sterile hospital room to the power of healing. God holds the ability to heal. Sometimes during trips to the hospital, all I could mumble was, "Jesus." That would be enough to shift my mind back to God. Upset and afraid, I knew I needed to continue to move forward.

There are times when I am looking around at situations. I've learned to look up and gaze at God's providential care.

Ephesians 6:18 (NLT)

Pray in the spirit at all times and on every occasion. Stay alert and be persistent in your prayers for all believers everywhere.

Praying is not a one and done event. Praying, being prayerful, or living a praying life is a continual action for the believer. Our continual prayers shift our thought life. Prayer shifts our perspective. Praying involves the vital action of listening. This is how we focus on the greatness of God and not the size of the problem, even when we are in a sterile hospital room.

Continue is defined as to persist in an activity or process. It means to carry on with something. We must pray continually, passionately, and consistently. This is how we fight spiritually. This is how we fasten our thoughts to God's truths. We don't pray from a place of defeat. We pray from a position of authority. God has all authority in His hands (Matthew 28:18). Even when I feel exhausted by the process of life, I keep praying. On happy and prosperous days, I continue to pray.

Prayer: *I will pray in season and out of season. I will stay alert and pray about everything. I will tell God the details of my life because He can handle it. Even when I am pulled in different directions today and juggling competing priorities, I will come to God in a posture of prayer.*

Philippians 4:6–7 (NLT)

"Don't worry about anything; instead, pray about everything. Tell God what you need, and thank him for all He has done.

Then you will experience God's peace, which exceeds anything we can understand. His peace will guard your hearts and minds as you live in Christ Jesus."

Questions: What situation is causing you stress today? What prayer of authority will shift your focus? God is in every detail today.

KEEPER

⌒

I remember the days of being a teenager in high school and dating a guy that was a college freshman. Of course, that boy crush was for all the wrong reasons—he was handsome and older than I was. That seemed like enough reason to say, "He's a keeper." Thirty years later we are blessed to still be together.

Think about your favorite movie. Any compelling movie has a full cast of characters, such as the leading role, supporting cast, villain, and extras. That boy crush that I had in high school evolved. After our wedding that crush made that guy one of the leading characters in the movie of my life. He became my husband.

We all need our squad—the person who holds us accountable, loves us, encourages us, challenges us, or makes us laugh uncontrollably. Esther in the Bible was a young girl with a cast of characters in her life. She began a life filled with hurt and trauma. Both her parents died while she was young. As an orphan, she was adopted by her cousin Mordecai. Mordecai became a keeper for Esther. Esther eventually became queen. She served an important role of rescuing God's chosen people from annihilation.

/ (NASB)

"...as bringing up Hadassah, that is Esther, his uncle's daugh-
..., for she had no father or mother. Now the young lady was
beautiful of form and face, and when her father and her mother
died, Mordecai took her as his own daughter."

Mordecai was a superhero for Esther. He kept Esther and raised
her as his very own daughter. The book of Esther shows that
no matter who compiles our cast of characters, we have only
one director: God. We can try to blur the lines, but God is in
complete control and the ultimate authority. That's what makes
Psalm 121:7 (ESV) reassuring: "The Lord will keep you from
all evil; he will keep your life."

Prayer: *Thank You, Lord, You are a keeper. As we go through the
years, we have different friends and family that make up our cast of
characters. We rest in the fact that You are the only director our movie
needs. Through the hard and painful moments Your providential care
covers us. You are concentrated on us all the time. Thank You for never
losing focus.*

Deuteronomy 8:3–4 (NLT)

"Yes, he humbled you by letting you go hungry and then feeding you with manna, a food previously unknown to you and
your ancestors. He did it to teach you that people need more
than bread for their life; real life comes by feeding on every
word of the Lord. For all these forty years your clothes didn't
wear out, and your feet didn't blister or swell."

Question: Can you give thanks to God for those who are in your squad today? Think about the impact they've had on your life.

POSITION

⌒

Life with my boys is loud. When my son comes home from college, the entire energy in the house changes. He is accustomed to constant stimulation. His college house with friends and roommates is loud. Most nights, I quietly watch the news or read before I cook dinner. During my son's last time home, watching anything was challenging. He was talking so loudly with his brother I could not even hear the TV. I just turned it off and relished the fact that he was home.

Every day, distractions come. Our world is noisy. We can become numb to the distractions and even start to crave them. There are so many items that pull our attention away, such as social media, friends, work, family, volunteering, podcasts, sports, TV, magazines, etc. The moment I sit to read or be still, the phone rings or I am reminded of an unfinished task. It is necessary to position ourselves to create clarity: clarity on how God is speaking; clarity on what God is speaking. Our breathless and frazzled lifestyles keep us in a swirl of forward motion, but what are we accomplishing? Being busy doesn't mean we are effective or productive. This constant motion keeps us numb to the needs around us.

2 Chronicles 20:3 (NLT)

"Jehoshaphat was alarmed by this news and sought the Lord for guidance...."

King Jehoshaphat was given alarming news. It was an interruption in his day. An army was marching towards him. He didn't overreact. The above verse shows that he sought the Lord for guidance. He prayed and waited for God to give instruction.

His prayer allowed him to hear the Lord. He started his prayer stating the power and authority of God. He focused on the fact that God was the ultimate ruler. This shifted Jehoshaphat's perspective from fear to rest.

Interruptions will come today. Someone is going to walk in your office right when you are about to work on a project. The interruption might come as a text that delivers unsettling news. Our response is to fasten our thoughts back to God. Thinking about God develops intimacy and growth in our relationship with Him because we are not relying on our own strength or problem solving. What a beautiful posture for King Jehoshaphat to model for his nation.

Prayer: *I will not limit myself to hearing God only during quiet time. Thank God You speak to Your children. In the same way I positioned and prepared my son for success in college, I will position myself to hear Your voice today. I don't want to just posture myself to have a productive day at work. I will position myself and seek Your guidance.*

Matthew 28:20 (NLT)

"Teach these new disciples to obey all the commands I have given you. And be sure of this: I am with you always, even to the end of the age."

Questions: What step can you take to position yourself to hear God today? What is He saying to you?

SUFFICIENT

⟨⟩

When trouble comes, we often wish those hard moments would disappear quickly. Life can swiftly bring difficult times that we want to be removed. We naturally want to lessen the impact of pain and grief. If we are sick, we visit the doctor seeking a prescription to rid us of the illness. Paul, an apostle in scripture, had a similar sentiment. He was facing a season with trial that he called a thorn in his flesh. He asked God three times to remove it.

2 Corinthians 12:8–10 (NIV)

"Three times I pleaded with the Lord to take it away from me. But he said to me, 'My grace is sufficient for you, for my power is made perfect in weakness.' Therefore I will boast all the more gladly about my weaknesses, so that Christ's power may rest on me. That is why, for Christ's sake, I delight in weaknesses, in insults, in hardships, in persecutions, in difficulties. For when I am weak, then I am strong."

The answer we need is not always to have the trial removed. In fact, you've been trusted with that trial. The trial might be the very thing that is drawing us closer to Christ. We might be spending more time praying and hearing His voice. A sincere prayer from a desperate heart keeps us dependent on Him. We yearn to be healed, and it seems that our requests are falling on deaf ears. God promises that His grace will be sufficient to carry us through the storms. When we move closer to God, we are moving further away from the enemy.

Paul's situation didn't change. It was given to him by the Lord. He knew that the strength of God was carrying him through the trial. We can rest knowing that what God provides is sufficient for us. The measure of how much He provides is sufficient. Sufficiency means there is enough.

Prayer: *God, thank You for Your adequate provision. Although my heart wants this trial or sickness to be removed, I rest in Your sufficient grace. God, thank You for being enough. During my present moments, awaken me to Your presence. When I seek Your face, it puts me in a posture to hear Your voice with clarity.*

Psalm 23:4 (NIV)

"Even though I walk through the darkest valley, I will fear no evil, for you are with me, your rod and your staff, they comfort me."

Questions: Do you believe that God's grace is sufficient? What else do you rely on in difficult times? God is enough. His provision is sufficient.

WISDOM

W here do you turn when a decision needs to be made? We often rely on wisdom from family or friends. We also lean solely into logic and reasoning. That's what makes us different from animals. We have the ability to reason. For example, medical intellect will explain to the heart patient why the heart valve is clogged. It is wisdom that guides the patient on how to take action and change their lifestyle behaviors.

Wisdom is incredibly valuable. We need Godly wisdom because it goes beyond intellect and reasoning. We need wisdom to apply the spiritual truths we've learned. As people, we are making decisions every day. We are our own CEO. We can take in information and choose to apply it or not apply it to our lives. King Solomon is known for his book of wisdom called Proverbs. He was known as one of the wisest men.

I King 3:5, 7–9 (NIV)

"...the Lord appeared to Solomon during the night in a dream, and God said, 'Ask for whatever you want me to give you.'

'Now, Lord my God, you have made your servant king in place of my father David. But I am only a little child and do not know how to carry out my duties. Your servant is here among the people you have chosen, a great people, too numerous to count or number. So give your servant a discerning heart to govern your people and to distinguish between right and wrong. For who is able to govern this great people of yours?'"

King Solomon asked for a discerning heart. A heart filled with God's wisdom. He needed an understanding mind. He recognized his weaknesses and limitations. He was a young king leading a large group of people. Solomon was humble in his request. Why didn't he ask for more money? I'm pretty sure I would have asked for more money. But what would it profit me to have more money and not any wisdom on how to manage the money? We all need the humility of Solomon, asking God to govern ourselves wisely as we navigate unsettling waters of life. The way God responded to Solomon inspires me.

I King 3:11–13 (NIV)

"So God said to him, 'Since you have asked for this and not for long life or wealth for yourself, nor have asked for the death of your enemies but for discernment in administering justice. I will do what you have asked. I will give you a wise and discerning heart, so that there will never have been anyone like you, nor will there ever be. Moreover, I will give you what you have not asked for—both wealth and honor—so that in your lifetime you will have no equal among kings.'"

Solomon was rewarded for asking for wisdom. My mom collaborated with other authors during the pandemic to write the book, *Age-Old Wisdom Sayings*. These are generational wise sayings taken from biblical principles. They are passed down through verbal conclusions that over time evolve into reliable truths. As a way to preserve these sayings from their ancestors, they pinned 155 wisdom sayings into a beautiful compilation. One of my favorite sayings is #73: "Make haste while the sun is shining." The biblical application is from Proverbs 10:5: Don't ignore opportunities. Do what you can while you can. Godly wisdom is a jewel of abundant living.

Prayer: *There are so many requests I have today, Lord. I pause and simply pray for Your wisdom as I go throughout today. Give me wisdom on how to apply Your truths to my life in every situation and in every decision. Thank You that I don't have to wander Earth in darkness because I have the mind of Christ (**I Corinthians 2:16**).*

Questions: What truth will you apply to a decision you are facing today? Are you ignoring any opportunities in your life? Where do you seek wisdom?

WILL

⁓

In a world filled with change and evolution, God's word is unchangeable. It is the same yesterday, today, and even in the future. The only constant in our lives is change. Scripture was written centuries ago, but remains relevant as we navigate life in the 21st century. As someone who studies the Bible, I often read the words *I will*.

When I see the word will, that means that there are no other options on the table. It is a definitive and decisive word. I will, is not the same as I am going to try. I will, is not the same as I think I can. I will are words of authority. They don't waver back and forth. God uses the words I will often when speaking through scripture.

Isaiah 40:31 (NLT)

"But those who trust in the Lord will find new strength. They will soar high on wings like eagles. They will run and not grow weary. They will walk and not faint."

Are you feeling weary today? Are you exhausted by life? Do you feel as if you are done fighting for your mental health? Fighting for the health of your marriage? Fighting for your physical health as you wage war against a medical diagnosis?

Fighting for financial prosperity? Fighting the enemy? Fighting for promotion? Fighting to have your reputation restored? Fighting to stay afloat? The word will, initiates action. God declares those who trust in the Lord *will* find new strength. It means God is going to do something or move in a mighty way on your behalf. I believe when I pray, it is not from a place of defeat. It is from a place of authority.

Isaiah 41:10 (NLT)

"Do not be afraid, for I am with you. Do not be discouraged for I am your God. I will strengthen you and help you. I will hold you up with my victorious right hand."

When God says I will, it shall be done. This is an intimate promise. God isn't sending an angel. He said, "I will be with you." God will strengthen you today and beyond. He will hold you up even when you face adversity and challenges. The Lord is always with you. (Psalm 16:8) The word of God is sure concerning you. Tether yourself to God's truths and not the deceptive voices we often hear in the world.

Prayer: *Lord, I pause today to thank You for being with me. Help me to live. I am weary and need to feel Your presence. Thank You for Your faithfulness. You never lie to me. You are a keeper of Your word. Your word is true and a source of comfort for me. I will bless You at all times. I cling to Your truths.*

Isaiah 55:11 (NLT)

"It is the same with my word. I send it out, and it always produces fruit. It will accomplish all I want it to, and it will prosper everywhere I send it."

Questions: Are you exhausted? Are you feeling weary? What promise from God brings you comfort today? God will strengthen you.

RESCUE

⟿

Lately, I've been praying frequently. Not only praying more, but posturing myself to hear God speak. I normally pray and list requests before God. Now I realize the need to just listen and linger. Listen for direction. Sometimes God speaks through a song, scripture, or a sunset during my evening walk. I am intentional about hearing His voice, especially during unsettling times of uncertainty. It's a gentle whisper or nudge. If I don't listen closely, I will miss Him speaking. The more time I spend with Him, the easier I find it to discern His voice.

Life brings days that are filled with smiles, giggles, and happiness. We wish those moments would last longer. You know, the days when you pinch yourself and wonder how long this happiness will last. When you go through hurt, it can leave such a sting you start looking for hurt everywhere.

We can experience loss in many different ways—loss of a routine, loss of control, loss of a loved one, loss of employment, or even loss of closeness with your child as they transition to a new chapter of life. Loss can feel like weights that keep being stacked on top of each other. The weight squeezes us and impacts our ability to breathe freely. Stress affects us physically, eventually leaving us feeling buried and compressed in losses.

Who can rescue us from pain and hurt? Who can restore what has been taken away?

In moments like this, I turn to King David, who was acquainted with loss. He also understood the power of being rescued. In Psalm 34:1, David commits to bless the Lord at all times. In the middle of that psalm, he addresses fear and troubles.

Psalm 34:17–19 (NLT)

"The Lord hears his people when they call to him for help. He rescues them from all their troubles. The Lord is close to the broken-hearted; he rescues those whose spirits are crushed. The righteous person faces many troubles, but the Lord comes to the rescue each time."

Here is our answer. The Lord will rescue us. We can commit to not stare constantly in the face of our circumstances. We can focus on the power of God to rescue us. God hears our prayers. He sees you. He is acquainted with your feelings. We are valued in His kingdom. God is near to the broken-hearted and those who are crushed with grief.

Prayer: *Thank You, God, that You are my deliverer. On days when I feel blue, please remind me how You have already rescued me. I am more than a conqueror because You rescued me. Thank You for overcoming the world and not abandoning me during life's struggles.*

John 16:33 (NLT)

"I have told you these things, so that in me you may have peace. In this world you will have trouble. But take heart! I have overcome the world."

Questions: What situation can you surrender today? How can you intentionally focus on the power of God to rescue you?

PROCLAIM

In the course of a day, we speak many words. If someone was able to collect all of those words, what would they hear? Words that are good or bad, positive or negative? Would they be words that spread fear or faith? We have the power to proclaim any number of words throughout the day. Our stories, experiences, pains, and triumphs can all be used to complain or proclaim the goodness of God.

My boys use social media and snap videos at lightning speed. They add it to their storyline. Sometimes without my permission, they will videotape me. I view the video, and I'm not always pleased. Then there are times I am laughing at my silly ways. We can quickly become mad and frustrated. The tone of our voice changes. The body language becomes defensive. These are all things we don't notice until it's played back to us in real time.

Whenever I ponder during the month of December, I think about one of the greatest proclamations made in history—the proclamation that the angel of the Lord gave to the shepherds.

Luke 2:10–11 (NLT)

"But the angel reassured them. 'Don't be afraid!' he said. 'I bring you good news that will bring great joy to all people. The Savior—yes, the Messiah, the Lord—has been born today in Bethlehem, the city of David!'"

This proclamation is the bedrock of the Christian faith. Proclaim means to declare or announce something that is considered important. We have that opportunity to declare the good news of the gospel, not just in December but throughout the year.

In the midst of uncertainty, we can leverage our words to provide a gift of hope and comfort for others. Giving a gift to someone doesn't have to cost money. We can offer a word that encourages. It's so effortless to join in on conversations that are negative. The intentionality of our choice of words should be directed in a more powerful and positive way. Our words are tiny seeds that are planted, watered, and over time bring forth a harvest. You will reap what you sow (Galatians 6:7).

Today, for example, we can proclaim the strength, holiness, unfailing love, grace, and mercy of Jesus. That will bring someone hope when evidence of circumstances paints a harsher reality. We don't have to depend on our own strength during the spicy times of life. Proclaiming that to someone takes the weight off their shoulders. Your kind words might remind them that they are not walking alone.

We can proclaim our identity in Jesus Christ. We are not defined by the season of life we are currently facing. We could be in a season of rebuilding, busyness with toddlers, tweens, or teenagers. We could be embarking on a season of loss and grief, addiction, health challenges, or a season of caregiving. These are only seasons and not our identity. God proclaims in scripture our true identity.

I Peter 2:9 (NLT)

"But you are not like that, for you are a chosen people. You are royal priests, a holy nation, God's very own possession…."

Prayer: *Lord, make me bold today to proclaim Your power, glory, and authority. Utilize me as an agent of change. Align my words during this season to declare Your greatness. Make me intentional with my daily proclamations even when I'm navigating hardships.*

I Corinthians 11:26 (NIV)

"For whenever you eat this bread and drink this cup, you proclaim the Lord's death until he comes."

Questions: What will you proclaim today? What is a kind word that you can share with someone else?

JOY

～

Think about the place that brings you happiness. Is it a sandy beach while you gaze at the ocean or possibly the mountains while you hike on a crisp morning? Does happiness come from an amber sky sunset, a pet, or a relationship? Maybe joy comes from you being curled up on the couch reading a good book, creating music, or playing a sport? The places that bring me joy are both the beach and the mountains. It is stimulating for our mental health to randomly reminisce about our happy places. It has a way of shifting our thoughts and resetting our focus.

I enjoy reading the book of Psalms. David was a key contributor in writing the psalms. The range of emotions he navigates seems very relevant to me. In Psalm 34, David was on the run. People were jealous of what he'd achieved. David pretended to be insane in front of the king to prevent the king murdering him. Eventually David finds himself in a cave, hiding. David achieved success, but was now isolated because of fear.

Have you ever locked yourself in a car, closet, or bathroom just to be secluded from others? I remember a season in my life where I felt like I was on a carnival carousel wanting to jump off so I could catch up to the velocity of life. Time was moving so quickly. I was stuck in my routine. It was starting to feel mundane. There was an illusion that everyone appeared to be moving forward except for me. I wanted to capture more time with my dad whom I had recently lost to cancer. I just wanted time to stop for a brief moment.

Psalm 34:1 (NLT)

"I will bless the Lord at all times. I will constantly speak his praises."

David, in the midst of running for his life and hiding, committed to praise the Lord. In our praise, our thankfulness, our gratitude, we are repositioned to hear the voice of God. I Thessalonians 5:16 (NLT) tells us to always be joyful. Now, we don't feel joy when we experience pain. Joy is an internal superpower to have in the midst of the pain. Internal joy comes only from God. Joy doesn't fluctuate based on circumstances. It's joy when we think about the sacrifice God made for us to have eternal life. Joy to be assured that God is in every detail of our life. Joy that God goes before us to preserve our life.

It's the blessed assurance that no matter what we experience here on Earth, it is only temporary pain. It reminds me of the pain of childbirth. You feel it (*all* of it), and then your pain turns to incredible delight over the birth of your newborn. The joy of the Lord gives us strength. We might not have happy circumstances or experiences, but we can have joy.

Prayer: *Lord, I realize that my everyday experiences won't always make me happy. I surrender to be still and know that in every circumstance You are God. Thank You for leaving the Holy Spirit. I surrender* *to walk in joy because no matter what I face today, You are with me. It brings me joy to think that You called my name and I ran out of darkness. Thank You for salvation.*

James 1:2 (NLT)

"Dear brothers and sisters, whenever trouble comes your way, let it be an opportunity for joy."

Question: What promise from God brings you joy? Spend time today remembering that promise.

CIRCUMSTANCES

The phone rang while I was standing on the sales floor working at a department store. In a flash of lightning, my world changed. My mom was calling to let me know my father was extremely sick. It was to the point that Hospice was at our home. I gathered my thoughts and mustered the energy to leave work. Tears streamed down my face. I eventually took the three-hour drive to be home with my father.

Within days my father transitioned to heaven. That death left my heart filled with grief. Initially, I felt disoriented. Death is final. The sting of that death never leaves. Celebrating the first holidays without Dad was tough. Father's Day, his birthday, and Christmas forced us to start creating new memories. I kept a voicemail he left on my phone for as long as I could. I would replay it just to hear his voice. If I smelled his cologne, it would trigger memories of my dad.

Circumstances in life can change in an instant. One phone call or knock at the door can disrupt the normal pattern of life. You can feel kicked in the gut and gasping for air. You want the world to stop turning but it doesn't. Suffering and sorrow happen in a fallen world.

I Thessalonians 5:18 (NIV)

"Give thanks in all circumstances; for this is God's will for you in Christ Jesus."

In the weeks following the funeral, giving thanks was not on my agenda. I felt angry that a faithful family that prayed and cried out to God lost their loved one. I now realize that healing comes in many forms. My prayers for healing were answered, just in a way that was completely different than I envisioned. Rubbing my father's arm and seeing him more peaceful gave me comfort. He endured a horrible and painful battle with cancer.

Our hearts of gratitude shouldn't fluctuate because our circumstances change. The scripture in Thessalonians tells us to give thanks *in* all things, not *for* all things. In the midst of the hardship and loss we can give thanks for the life lived. It's the tough and spicy moments of life that draw us into deeper intimacy with Christ. Surrendering to God means giving it all to Him. Even when a circumstance disrupts the natural rhythm of life.

Prayer: *Not every circumstance feels good. If I had a flag, God, I would want it flying at half-staff today. Even with those raw feelings, I trust the plan You have for my life. I thank You for the circumstances that are seeds for growth. I am Your image bearer, and I want to thank You for open and closed doors today. Thank You for the happy and sad moments. I know You are not surprised by any of them. You can safely carry me through each of them.*

Habakkuk 3:17–19 (NLT)

"Even though the fig trees have no blossoms, and there are no grapes on the vines; even though the olive crop fails, and the fields lie empty and barren; even though the flocks die in the fields, and the cattle barns are empty, yet I will rejoice in the Lord!

I will be joyful in the God of my salvation! The Sovereign Lord is my strength! He makes me as surefooted as a deer, able to tread upon the heights."

Question: What circumstance are you navigating today? God is with you. Focus on what remains today versus what's been lost.

AWARE

A re you aware of how strong you are? We have moments of weakness but also lifetimes of strength. Friends might have to point out your strength. Every time I've been asked in an interview what my strengths are, I hesitate to answer the question. People take tests or assessments to uncover their strengths. They hire executive coaches to show them how to use those strengths to take a bold step forward.

During the tough and complex times of life, strength is on display. Parents come home exhausted from work yet have energy to roll around on the floor with the kids. We don't know we have it in us. Strength is pressed out of us through trials. A young adult student matriculates through layers of learning to earn that coveted degree. Time spent studying isn't glamorous but that student is harnessing an internal strength to stay focused. Are you aware of your strength?

Are you aware of the calling or purpose for your life? Purpose is not to be confused with daily assignments. There is a reason you were born during this time in history. God is not going to waste any of the experiences that you've had in your life. Every situation, good or bad, is a tailored design of a unique story. God's workmanship is marvelous (Psalm 139:14). His thoughts toward you are precious.

We can read and skim through certain scripture passages. Then there are times when we are made aware of a certain text because it's so relevant to our current life happenings. That scripture is highlighted in our hearts. As we read the Bible, we might think that it doesn't apply to our life. But the word of God is full of present promises that we need to be aware of.

Matthew 28:20 (NLT)

"...And be sure of this: 'I am with you always, even to the end of the age.'"

Everywhere we go today, God is with us. Wherever I am, He shows up. Wherever life takes you, God has already prepared the way. It could be a family gathering, at work, shopping, in the barbershop, anywhere we are. Be awakened and aware of that truth today. Draw courage from that truth. The power of God is hovering over you today. His love overtakes you.

I remember riding a subway in New York when I saw a woman crying. She sat silently but tearfully. I was led to place my hand on her shoulder. Now, touching someone on a New York subway is not normal activity. But I wanted to, in some small way, let her know that I saw her. I wanted her to be aware that she wasn't alone. How can you shine today so that God can receive glory?

We must be aware of God in us. It's not me and God, it's God in me. Awaken to your conviction and calling. We are not here just to soak up air. We have a purpose. If you aren't clear about it, pray and ask God.

Matthew 5:16 (NKJV)

"You are the light of the world. A city that is set on a hill cannot be hidden."

Prayer: *Today, I will present myself to the world full of confidence in the power of God. Wherever I walk, He is with me. I will move throughout today fully aware of that truth. I won't shrink in fear but rise to every challenge in faith.*

Matthew 5:16 (NIV)

"In the same way, let your light shine before others, that they may see your good deeds and glorify your Father in heaven."

Question: What one action of confidence can you take today because you are aware that God is with you?

CLOSE

⁓

Most headlines that start the national or local news are negative. The news might end with a positive story after twenty-five minutes of negativity. That, unfortunately, develops a level of sadness within my heart. When I see overt hate, violence, or corruption, it upsets me. It's one of the reasons I stopped watching the news. Raising my boys, I didn't want our home to be filled with jaw-dropping news stories.

There are times in life where God's silence makes me think He is far away. Why isn't He speaking? It is hard to trust an invisible God. Then I read Colossians 1:15 that sweetly says, "Christ is the visible image of the invisible God." It confirmed that God isn't silent or away from me. God is always speaking. The question is, am I in a position to hear His voice?

As a child, if we had a test in school, the teacher was silent. They would proctor the exams to ensure there was no cheating. Even though the teacher was silent, their presence was still in the room. When God feels far away or silent, He is close. That truth is not going to be based on how I feel; it's based on what God declares in His word.

I've learned to sit still and check in to evaluate how I'm feeling. I call this a purposeful pause. I take it throughout the day to see what my body needs. Sometimes it's a walk or a nap. Walking away from a project to take some deep breaths refreshes me.

Psalm 34:18 (NIV)

"The Lord is close to the broken-hearted and saves those who are crushed in spirit."

Psalm 34:18 (MSG)

"If your heart is broken, you'll find God right there; if you're kicked in the gut, he'll help you catch your breath."

Will today be a day that you are crushed with grief? Do you feel kicked in the gut?

God is here and He is near. We can raise our level of awareness to His presence by just simply calling on the name, "Jesus." The power of the name Jesus puts Him right in the center of our grief. Grief isn't always felt because someone died. Having a student leave home for college can bring grief. The loss of a marriage requires some time to grieve. A mom realizing that she will not birth any other children can cause a sense of loss as well. It is ok to not be ok. Check in with yourself to understand how you are feeling.

Calling God's name moves us closer to Him. It refocuses our thoughts. The enemy will distract us with daily activities to keep us away from feeling His presence. Today, God will be your source of power, courage, and wisdom. If you are feeling weak throughout today, remember God is strong. His words are true. He promises never to leave you.

Hebrews 13:5 (NIV)

"...Never will I leave you; never will I forsake you."

Prayer: *When I am drowning with anxiety and sadness, thank You, God, for reminding me that You are close. I will seek You today. I know I can walk through fire and not come out smelling like smoke. Your angels have charge over me today. In the light of You, I have safety. I draw from Your strength through every success or struggle I encounter today.*

Questions: What distracts you today? What action can you take to be assured of God's presence?

SOLITUDE

Parenting does not frequently provide times of solitude. My toddler boys would cling to my legs. I remember cooking dinner while holding my oldest son on my hip. That was the only way to finish any project. The moment my husband would come home from work, I would run out of the house (literally). This stay-at-home mom needed a break. I craved space for solitude. Being a parent requires a constant demand of your time. It's also incredibly rewarding.

I found ways to find snippets of time to myself. I would put the boys in the stroller and go for a walk. Although they went with me, they would be lulled to sleep. Oh, how I remember the joy of naptime. Life outside with nature is the greatest mobile for a baby. The warm sun, swaying trees, and fluttering birds kept them occupied. Morning walks allow me the opportunity to clear my head and find solitude.

I've noticed that the birds are noisier than in the past. Maybe I am just more attentive to their chirps. I'm up early enough to hear the birds' morning chorus. Some birds' calls in the early morning are different from their calls during the day. It's a gracious greeting introducing a new day. The sound is loud, lively, and frequent. It's a harmonious sound.

Birds minister to me. They fly effortlessly. When storms come, they innately move away from harm. They fly with such freedom. They don't have refrigerators or pantries to store food. They rely on daily provision. Jesus talks about birds in scripture.

Matthew 6:25–27 (NLT)

"That is why I tell you not to worry about everyday life—whether you have enough food and drink, or enough clothes to wear. Isn't life more than food, and your body more than clothing? Look at the birds. They don't plant or harvest or store food in barns, for your heavenly Father feeds them. And aren't you far more valuable to him than they are? Can all your worries add a single moment to your life?"

The solitude of my morning walks allows me to focus. I'm able to set my priorities for the day ahead. Jesus encouraged His disciples to look at the birds. Pause, breathe, and watch the birds. Birds provided a backdrop of Godly provision. We don't have to worry. Humans are wired to worry. About 85% of what we worry about never happens per Melanie Greenberg, a clinical psychologist in Mill Valley, California. Shift your focus. In stillness and solitude we can recalibrate our world.

Self-defeating thoughts are little seeds. The more we mull them over in our mind, the more they grow. If someone loses their job, they might make a generalized statement of, "I'm never going back to work." A student might repeat, "I'll never pass this test." These broad statements are untrue but they started with a seed of self-doubt. When speaking, ask yourself—is this true? Doubt and nonbelief swiftly transform into worry and torment.

Prayer: *Today, I will create solitude to hear God speak. I will listen to His voice. I will redirect my thoughts. I am God's beloved child. He cares for me. I will let heaven fill my thoughts today.*

Colossians 3:2 (NLT)

"Let heaven fill your thoughts. Do not think only about things here on earth."

Questions: How do you carve space for solitude? What did you learn during your space of solitude?

CHOICE

⌒

A colleague once told me, "Control the controllables." In an ever-evolving world, there isn't much we can control. We learned hard lessons in 2020 during a global pandemic that initially ushered a new silence and chaos into the world. Every norm of society was impacted. Social inequities were revealed. New ways of interacting with others, educating students, and buying groceries arose. Our lives were disrupted. One of the only controllables was our response to the change.

In our quest to control, we will be frustrated. We can't be in control of every situation, but we can control our response. Change is our new norm. The only thing that stays the same is change. Because of this, we will cycle through numerous emotions throughout the day. Life is unpredictable. This is the reason why I cherish my sacred morning routine. Before I read any news headline, I want to create my own headline—one where I choose to show calm in the midst of chaos.

Today you have a choice in front of you. A choice to live or to die. A choice to believe God or disregard everything He says. A choice for our brain to deliver thoughts of peace or destruction. A choice for our spoken words to uplift or tear down. What will you choose today?

Walking through the unknown is scary. I felt this when my identical twin sister was diagnosed with cancer. She became ill quickly. I used FaceTime to communicate with her. She was finally rushed into emergency surgery. I wanted more control over the situation. A talk with my mom lifted me from a place of worry. She simply said, "Renee will be alright." With those four spoken words, I had a new perspective, enough to keep fighting and praying for my sister. I initially felt like a wounded warrior. When my mom spoke, I felt a new strength.

In uncertain times, you can't see what's in front of you. You rely heavily on past experiences, even when they've been traumatic. Relying on our past provides a filtered wisdom. We see everything through the lens of our past hurts. Facing new challenges can leave us feeling overwhelmed, devastated, crushed, or torn.

I Peter 5:7 (NLT)

"Give all your worries and cares to God, for he cares about you."

When someone is in the hospital, I put this scripture on a poster and place it in their room. There is a choice to be made, clutching onto worry or releasing our cares into the arms of someone who can shoulder all of it. Much of what we encounter in life is too heavy for us to carry. Are you feeling a weight on your shoulders today? With each thought, surrender that weight. Take a breath. Let go of it. It's weighing you down or possibly slowing your progress.

Prayer: *I choose today to be full of faith and not fear. I choose to live. Through God's strength I will take that small step forward. I want to see progress versus perfection. Thank God for providing me a choice. I choose you.*

Hebrews 12:1 (NLT)

"Therefore, since we are surrounded by such a huge crowd of witnesses to the life of faith, let us strip off every weight that slows us down, especially the sin that so easily trips us up. And let us run with endurance the race God has set before us."

Question: How will you respond today to life's perplexing situations?

ACCEPT

⌒

How many times have you interacted with someone you weren't fond of? Maybe it's someone with whom you don't share the same values. I bet it is more than you can count. There are instances when the person we aren't fond of sits within our own families, maybe even in our house.

Interacting with others is challenging, but it's the reality of living as a human. We are constantly interacting with people. Some people are just annoying, rude, or mean. No one wants to admit those feelings, but they exist. I've had unpleasant experiences many times.

I remember helping a customer purchase a gift during the busy Christmas shopping season. She came to me in a flurry. The store was packed, and she was in a rush. I calmly greeted her, and she questioned why I wasn't speaking the familiar language of that city. I explained as best I could that I spoke only English. She gave me a finger gesture that wasn't welcoming and stormed off. That was rude and unpleasant.

It is easy to be nice to those who are friendly or share my values. Recently, I came face to face with someone who rubbed me the wrong way. We held completely different beliefs. Thinking differently than me wasn't the issue. It was the way she presented her beliefs to me. After the interaction, I just asked God for clarity on how to move forward with her condescending attitude. I knew I was walking in the purpose God gave me. I didn't understand why there was so much opposition. After asking God, His words were simple: Accept her humanity. I couldn't believe God said, "Accept her." Why couldn't she accept me? I didn't expect that answer from God.

We can begin daily interactions with people based on our belief system, traditions, judgment, and criticism. Now imagine starting all human interactions from an authentic place of acceptance, choosing not to judge based on appearance or a belief system. I don't have to agree with someone's lifestyle choices. Accepting their humanity is the critical first step.

Our world constantly generalizes people into groups based on their identities. Generalizing people into groups provides a way to lump us together and predict behaviors, but it robs our uniqueness. The enemy looks for ways to divide us. During an election year, you taste the tension in the air between different political parties. We can't allow that division to happen in our homes, places of worship, or offices.

Romans 15:7 (NLT)

"So accept each other just as Christ has accepted you; then God will be glorified."

God accepted us when we were far away from Him. God accepted a life not characterized as "godly." God accepted us when we didn't agree with Him. God accepted us while we were still sinners (Romans 5:8). We can accept others because He first accepted us.

Psalm 141:2 (NLT)

"Accept my prayer as incense offered to you, and my upraised hands as an evening offering."

Prayer: *God, penetrate my heart to accept others, even when I don't agree with them. I am grateful that You accepted me. May I approach each interaction today with humility. I want the power of God displayed in my relationships today.*

Question: Who do you need to accept today? Accepting someone does not equate to agreeing with them. You can accept someone and still disagree with them.

ADORE

⌒

Ever since I was a little girl, I have always adored babies. Their chubby cheeks, perfect lips, little hands and toes bring a smile to my face. If I see a baby now while I am out shopping, I will stop and stare. It's their giggles, gurgles, and innocence that make me happy. This world can be so cruel. Babies remind me of a fresh start. It's not just me who feels this way. My husband is also passionate about children. He can make crying babies suddenly start to laugh. They are instantly drawn to him. We are blessed with our two sons.

It's one thing to stare at kids from a distance. Other people's kids aren't coming home with you. Bursts of time spent with children bring me back to reminiscing about all the years as a stay-at-home mom. That was tough work. There are times when our own kids make us smile and scream all within the same hour. Having the doctor place them in my arms for the first time is quite a memorable moment for me. There was an instant adoration for those baby boys.

The song, "O Come All Ye Faithful," is sung mostly during the Christmas season. I really enjoy the rendition by Luther Vandross. In that song are the lyrics, "Oh come let us adore him." I find that I sing that song throughout the entire year. That song tells us to adore God. Come and behold God's greatness. When I am in complete confusion over another phone call or text announcing death or any other horrific news, I try to quickly bring my mind back to adoring God—revelling in His ability not to make any errors.

It's a place mentally where I adore and lift Him higher than my own questions and confusion. I feel peace settle in my heart. I don't push down the raw emotions of the moment. I allow myself to be sad or angry. But I also choose not to stay in that space and dwell on it. I release the situation to God through prayer.

As I write this chapter, I just received the shocking news of my cousin's death. A precious life lived transitioned to heaven at such a young age, gone too soon from Earth, yet safe and secure in heaven. Her social media profile quickly became a tribute to her memory. Her last-shared photos are now pieces of her legacy.

My aunt is resilient. She knows the sting of death. She's a woman who buried two sons and a husband, yet survives with strength and resolve. Who can contend with such loss? When my father died, her words comforted me in a unique way. I knew she was familiar with the unbearable and gut-wrenching pain of death. She told me I would have my father's memory triggered in my heart unannounced. For example, I found myself crying just seeing a granddad playing baseball outside with his grandson. My aunt warned me not to stay there, dwelling on the past. She didn't want me meditating only on his loss. She understood that staying there in my thoughts would eventually lead to continued feelings of grief, loneliness, and eventually depression. There was a deepening of my faith after his death.

I Chronicles 29:11 (NLT)

"Yours, O Lord, is the greatness, the power, the glory, the victory, and the majesty. Everything in the heavens and on earth is yours, O Lord, and this is your kingdom. We adore you as the one who is over all things."

During times that sting in life, let's remind ourselves of the one who is over all things. He adores us. He has time to hear us. God fervently listens to us. We are precious to God. Our current reality is not our final destination. We can easily adore the wrong people, relationships, careers, and stuff in our lives. Our affection should be attached to God, whose ways are higher than our ways. God's thoughts are higher than our thoughts. God sees beyond the current circumstances. He is the ultimate authority. God has the final say. God sustains even as we travel over troubled waters.

Prayer: *I surrender control over my life to You, Lord. I will listen today to hear Your instructions. God, thank You for the peace of knowing You adore me. I am precious to You. I will remember Your love for me. When life hurts, I still love and adore You. Thank You for this great love.*

Psalm 121:5 (NLT)

"The Lord himself watches over you! The Lord stands beside you as your protective shade."

Question: What troubles your heart today? Take a moment to ruminate on the lavish love God has for you (Exodus 20:6). God laid down His son's (Jesus') life so that you may live eternally with Him.

PRESERVE

⌒

A few years back I had an urgent medical situation with my heart. The heart is so precious. The heart has so many responsibilities; for example, pumping oxygenated blood through the body. It's obvious why this scripture shows up in the book of Proverbs.

Proverbs 4:23 (NLT)

"Above all else, guard your heart, for it affects everything you do."

In times of calm or times of chaos, we must protect and preserve the place that affects everything we do. Preserve your heart. Also preserve your peace. Receiving peace isn't dependent on the situations we are facing. God offers peace while we are in the storm. As we are cruising through the routines of life, God offers peace. During gut-wrenching moments of life, God offers peace. When life feels uncertain and scary, God offers peace. If we don't know the next step or have a question, God offers peace.

When Jesus was on Earth, He experienced a storm while He and His disciples were in a boat. They experienced the same storm on the same night, but they had different reactions. Jesus slept in peace on the boat while the disciples were shouting and frantic. With this parable I learned that Jesus is always in the boat with me. I won't steer off course keeping my eyes and thoughts focused on His calm and authority.

We can experience the type of peace that keeps us at rest during the storm. We can also pragmatically preserve our peace throughout the day by limiting our distractions. Everything beeps when we receive status updates, new email, new deliveries, a phone call, or any other notification. Utilizing the Do Not Disturb function on our devices is a way to preserve our peace and focus intently on the priority of the moment.

Life is fleeting. We must preserve the history of our families through capturing our elders' recipes, cultural traditions, stories, famous sayings, and historical items that exist in their home. When my aunt died, her recipe for these delicious brownies left the family. During every family gathering she would bake those brownies. I miss her chocolate- and nut-filled brownies that would melt in my mouth.

We can also work to preserve a lifestyle of gratitude. Again, life can be distracting, and we can fall into complaining and discontentment even when there is so much to be thankful for. Focus on what you have instead of what you don't possess. Whatever has our attention grows larger in our imagination. During the moments of stress and frustration today, find three reasons to have gratitude. It can be as simple as gratitude for a sunny sky.

Prayer: *I am aware that I have the ability to preserve my peace by refocusing my thoughts. Silencing the voices of negative and self-defeating thoughts today will help me preserve my peace. I am thankful for a fresh start. Thank You, God, for life today.*

John 14:27 (NLT)

"I am leaving you with a gift—peace of mind and heart. And the peace I give is a gift the world cannot give. So, don't be troubled or afraid."

Questions: What are three things you are thankful for today? What is a way to limit distractions in your life today?

HOPE

~~~~~~~

During this week I've felt a range of emotions. Within one week I've felt stress, anger, fear, anxiety, happiness, and relief. Some of those emotions were all felt on the same day. I am surrounded by turbulent activity. As I'm writing this, our global world is navigating the pandemic of 2020. There are disruptions in life that are impacting not only me but also the world around me. I can't keep carrying the heavy weight of stress that seems permanently attached to my shoulders.

I am talking with others who are feeling defeated. I've had more friends lose their mother during this year. Those who still have their parents feel guilt. Food distribution lines are long as people are adjusting to food insecurity, many for the first time. Again, those who have pantries full of food feel guilt. How do we do more to help those who are less fortunate? I know life won't always be this way, but right now it is discouraging. There are days and days of protest. I'm starting not to recognize the world I'm currently living in. This ominous feeling in the air is felt by many.

Jeremiah was affectionately called the weeping prophet. He wept and lamented over the rebellion and pride in the land he lived. Yet, in the midst of the adversity, he found hope.

Lamentations 3:20–24 (NLT)

"I will never forget this awful time, as I grieve over my loss.

Yet I still dare to hope when I remember this:

> The faithful love of the Lord never ends! His mercies never cease.
>
> Great is his faithfulness; his mercies begin afresh each morning.
>
> I say to myself, 'The Lord is my inheritance; therefore, I will hope in him!'"

Some events that happen in our life we will never forget. Jeremiah didn't push away feelings. He knew the days were awful. He was grieving over his losses. Did you notice that Jeremiah dared to have hope? There are moments where we shed tears through difficulties. We experience hearts that are faint. The darkness becomes a perfect backdrop for the power and glory of God to be revealed. We don't have to wish for God to do more. What the Lord has already done is final and it is enough (Ecclesiastes 3:14).

When we are consumed with life, we can lament before God and find hope in Him. We can lift our hands in worship and praise to recalibrate the atmosphere around us. Silence the negative voices and lean in to hear God. In a gentle whisper, text, song, or scripture we can be reoriented in a new direction. Satan is the father of all lies, yet we put our hope in Jesus.

Prayer: *God, I surrender my frailties to You. I will choose not to think about my own abilities but find hope in the power of Your strength.*

Thank You for new mercies today. I have an expectation, a hope that You will be my guide today. I will choose not to worry about tomorrow's trouble because You will take care of all that comes to me today. I hope in You, Jesus.

Psalm 71:5 (NLT)

"O Lord, you alone are my hope. I've trusted you, O Lord, from childhood."

Question: How can you dare to have hope today? Write one scripture on an index card that speaks of God's hope. Don't give up; take one step forward by faith.

EXPECTATION

⌒

A renovation in any part of the house is loud, dusty, and full of expectation. I remember the renovation of my kitchen. After twenty years living in our house, we decided to completely gut it and rebuild. For my kitchen to become more beautiful, it was deconstructed only to be reconstructed. That happens in our lives too. Some days can feel torn down and flattened, similar to a kitchen on demo day. Who we become after construction is a stronger, confident, and restored person.

During the kitchen construction we lived with expectation. There were many moving parts with this renovation—design, demo, cabinets, appliances, countertops, permits, inspections, etc. I didn't realize how much dust appears when you renovate. It was everywhere. I was washing dishes in my bathroom sink. We grilled outside most nights. The house was in disarray. It was quite unsettling.

I worked from home, and there were people constantly in and out of the house. They didn't close the door. At night I would find lizards that slipped in through those open doors. It was a mess. I held onto the 3D picture presented to us by our designer. Thankfully, that was a visible image of what was to come. Expectation helps sustain you through the messy middle of life. The middle of a marriage, the middle of a project, the middle of completing a degree. What messy middle part of life are you in today?

Reading the Bible becomes that visible image of what we can expect in the future. It strengthens us as we spend time filled with the hope of a new day. A day when sickness, sorrow, pain, and death are removed (Revelation 21:4). God will make all things new. God makes us strong and steady, not just in our eternal life but while we are here on Earth. We can expect a day when our world will be freed from death and decay (Romans 8:21). We can live with great expectation. Although our present bodies grow weary, we have hope.

Romans 8:18–19 (NLT)

"Yet what we suffer now is nothing compared to the glory he will give us later. For all creation is waiting eagerly for that future day...."

Waiting through that construction process was frustrating. But every phase was necessary. I have a remodeled kitchen that I use constantly. Now that years have passed since the renovation, I'm ready to do it again in another room of the house.

When we go through tough seasons of life, we look over our shoulder, waiting for another mishap. Christ is walking with us through every season of life. Because of that, we have an assurance that grace provided is sufficient. We also don't need to expect God loving us less. Nothing we do today can take away or add to His love for us (Ecclesiastes 3:14). God lavishes His love on His children. We can love because He first loved us.

Prayer: *I live with great expectations today. I am eager to see how You will work in my life. There are moments when I don't know how to pray for myself. I can expect the Holy Spirit to pray for me in a way that can't be expressed in words. I expect Your love today. I expect Your protection today. This day is a gift. Thank You, Lord, for new mercy.*

Romans 8:28 (NLT)

"And we know that God causes everything to work together for the good of those who love God and are called according to his purpose for them."

Power of One links each word together. This book was written from the heart of an author with expectations, an expectant hope that allows me to see beyond negative news headlines and tough seasons of life. It is a hope that brings joy and peace in the midst of adversity, an eternal hope that sustains. We can rest assured that God cannot lie. He can be trusted to keep His promises. I have an anticipated hope that allows me to envision the day I see my deceased loved ones again. I pray this hope finds you today and settles in your heart. Trusting in God allows hope to overflow in your life (Romans 15:13).

Question: What do you expect God to do in your life today? Expect greatness from Him. Even when we can't see Him, He is working.

ABOUT THE AUTHOR

Roslyn Rice

Roslyn is innovative, curious, and influential. She has a global mission to inspire the world. Roslyn intentionally strives to encourage humans through the sticky parts of life. She's provided inspiration for decades through blogging, mentoring, and public speaking. She embraces storytelling and humor to pull readers in and bravely inspire them. Roslyn is unequivocally confident that Christ has sustained her through the ebbs and flows of life.

Roslyn is Co-founder and CEO of DPI, LLC, a business management firm focusing on diversity and inclusion solutions for organizations. Earlier in her career she spent twenty-five years as a retail professional, leading teams and managing multi-million dollar accounts. She coauthors the blog, Double Portion Inspiration, with her identical twin sister. Roslyn is a leader and board chairperson at her local church. Roslyn and her husband, Tyjuan, reside in South Florida and have two sons, Tyler and Joshua.

Do you know someone navigating a season of loss?

Give them the gift of *Power of One: Finding Hope in the Midst of Struggle*. Each word will support uplifting their spirit during the spicy and painful moments of life.

AVAILABLE WHERE BOOKS ARE SOLD

Life transitions happen swiftly. Roslyn is here to motivate and encourage during life's toughest moments. There are multiple ways to connect as she fulfills her global mission to inspire others. Roslyn and her twin sister, Renee, offer a double dose of inspiration on their blog.

Blog: doubleportioninspiration.blogspot.com

Self-care starts with taking time for yourself. This blog is the perfect place to be still, have faith, take a breath, and laugh.

Website: DPI2.com
Email: roslyn@dpi2.com
Instagram: @doubleportion
Twitter: @doubleportionin
Facebook: DoublePortionInspiration
LinkedIn: https://www.linkedin.com/in/roslyn-rice/

HEARTS to be **HEARD**

Giving a Voice to Creativity!

With every donation, a voice will be given to
the creativity that lies within the hearts of
our children living with diverse challenges.

By making this difference, children that may
not have been given the opportunity to have their
Heart Heard will have the freedom to create
beautiful works of art and musical creations.

Donate by visiting

HeartstobeHeard.com

We thank you.

Made in the USA
Columbia, SC
03 September 2021